THE BIBLE AS
TRUTH

THE BIBLE AS TRUTH

MUSINGS ABOUT EVOLUTION JESUS, HELL AND SALVATION

JOHN VALADE

The Bible As Truth by John Valade, M. Div.
Copyright © 2022 by John Valade
All Rights Reserved.
ISBN: 978-1-59755-724-5
Published by: ADVANTAGE BOOKS™
Longwood, Florida, USA
www.advbookstore.com

This book and parts thereof may not be reproduced in any form, stored in a retrieval system or transmitted in any form by any means (electronic, mechanical, photocopy, recording or otherwise) without prior written permission of the author, except as provided by United States of America copyright law.

Unless otherwise indicated, Scripture quotations are taken from the Holy Bible, ***New International Version***®, NIV®. Copyright © 1973, 1978, 1984, 2011 by Biblica, Inc.™ Used by permission of Zondervan. All Rights Reserved.

Scripture quotations marked (KJV) are taken from The Holy Bible ***King James Version*** and are public domain.

Scripture quotations marked (NRSV) are taken from The Holy Bible ***New Revised Standard Version***, copyright © 1989 the Division of Christian Education of the National Council of the Churches of Christ in the United States of America. Used by permission. All rights reserved.

Library of Congress Catalog Number: 2023936040

Name: Valade, John, Author
Title: ***The Bible As Truth***
John Valade
Advantage Books, 2023
Identifiers: ISBN Paperback: 9781597557245, eBook: 9781597557351
Subjects: Christian Life: Inspirational

First Printing: May 2023
23 24 25 26 27 28 10 9 8 7 6 5 4 3 2

Introduction

Who am I, and why am I writing a book about the Bible?

I was a strange kid who never quite fit in. It didn't help that I was a bit shy and rather bookish. In fact, finding me during lunches and any free time at school was easy. I was in the library. Yes, I was *that* kid. I was a geek long before it was cool.

From the age of ten I have been interested in faith, religion, science (especially biology and astronomy) and technology. As a result, I have military and college training in electronics repair, a university Certificate in Data Processing, a Bachelor's Degree in Religious Education and a Master's Degree in Divinity specializing in Pastoral Ministry.

My parents were nominally Roman Catholic, and going to Mass was a constant as I was growing up. Something changed for me, however, when the Gideon's Society showed up at our school when I was in Grade 5. They handed each of us students a very small New Testament.

The King James version was a little tough on a young reader, but I waded my way through it anyway. What I found compelling as a 10-year-old, if you can believe it, was the introductory page that listed the 10 Commandments. With the help of a dictionary I managed to figure out what "covet" meant, but I had a bit more trouble with the concept of "adultery." (Hey, I was only 10 years old, and this was 1971.) My dad's "helpful" definition was "unfaithfulness in love," whatever *that* meant.

What struck my young mind, however, was how *sensible* those laws are. In a way, this was my first introduction to sociology. It seemed to me at the time that you could not have a livable civilization without rules like that. Respect for the family unit, respect for the broader society, respect for neighbors and their property and respect for other families' members made sense. These all seemed to be wrapped up in how respect for God needs to be worked out among human beings. Our society ignores those basic rules at its own peril.

And then there was the idea of God Himself. At first I learned about Him from my parents, especially in my mother's worship and prayer. Eventually I came to have a vague sense of God's handiwork in the incredible variety of life-forms and astronomical phenomena, which I studied in and out of class.

By my mid-teens however, neither my only sibling nor my parents seemed interested in going to church services. I not only kept going, but I became a leader in my Catholic high school's religion club. At the age of sixteen I encountered the work of the Worldwide Church of God and their leader, Herbert W. Armstrong.

Herbert Armstrong and company raised questions about Catholic doctrines like the eternal virginity of Mary by pointing out uncomfortable facts from the Bible, such as the four named half-brothers of Jesus[i] and the unnamed sisters (at least two, but probably more). They also insisted on a celibate priesthood, which was strange since Jesus healed Peter's mother-in-law[ii], and that in one letter Paul notes that Peter and other apostles get to travel with their wives[iii] on their missionary journeys.

They also had me wondering about the relationship between Old Testament law and grace, particularly about why churches meet on Sunday rather than the biblical Sabbath. I also came to wonder whether the Bible actually teaches that unrepentant human beings will burn in an eternal tormenting fire and therefore suffer forever. More on that later.

After I joined the military I did fellowship with the Worldwide Church of God for about forty years. In the late 1980's the founder of that church died, and his successors began researching their unique and sometimes heretical doctrines. By the late 1990's the denomination began overturning or discarding almost all of their unique doctrines and then their unique practices, such as meeting on the Old Testament Holy Days.

I began to suspect that it would be necessary to investigate our own previous and "new" doctrines and practices with an open yet critical mind to determine whether they made biblical sense. I came to see that the doctrinal changes were necessary to match the Bible's doctrines of grace and the triune nature of God. However, I also sensed that there was no biblical or doctrinal necessity to change our unique meeting times to match Sunday, Christmas and Easter.

I eventually went to Canadian Bible College and Briercrest Biblical Seminary to try to resolve many of the questions raised by that organization in my mind. It was a great experience to be in dialogue with accomplished theological thinkers and biblical scholars. My mind opened up, and so did my heart. We did not always agree, but the openness to discussion among biblical scholars and theologians was a refreshing change after a stultifying brief university experience.

Table of Contents

John Valade, M. Div.

1

Modern Science and the Bible

My dad had his own small library, mostly stocked with science and science fiction books. The Life Nature Library was a constant in my childhood and teens. Much of the research for primary school science class essays came from our own home library, and I grew up to love both science and science fiction.

I have always loved learning about how things work, and science was my favourite subject. For instance I was the only Grade 5 student in my science class who wrote essays about Gregor Johann Mendel's work as a pioneer of the science of Genetics or about Cepheid Variable pulsating stars. More about Mendel a bit later.

We moved to the province of Quebec when I was in Grade 6, and I usually found myself enrolled in Roman Catholic schools, where my best subjects were Religion and Science. (The only nickname that ever stuck to me more than a few days was "professor.") Okay, perhaps not Physics so much, but I did well in Chemistry and particularly well in Biology. I was the only Grade 9 student in Grade 11 Biology, and came out with the 2nd highest grade in my class.

It was during Biology class that I came to the conclusion that the "theory" of evolution was not scientific, or even realistic. Remember Gregor Mendel? He actually did experiments to determine the frequency of trait transmission between generations.[iv] He came up with laws of genetic trait distribution based on his theory of dominant and recessive genes. He published his work in 1866, but it was ignored by the scientific community for almost 35 years.

It was "rediscovered" in 1900, long after Charles Darwin became the darling of the world of science with his *On the Origin of Species,* published in 1859.

Even in Grade 9 the inconsistencies between Mendel's scientific research on genetic inheritance and Darwin's speculative hypothesis of mutation and natural selection made me realize that Mendel was on a a far more scientific foundation than Darwin. Why anyone would try to graft Mendel's work onto Darwin's is still puzzling to me to this day.

In my opinion, if Mendel had been published and widely distributed first Darwin would have been laughed out of the scientific community for spouting nonsense. The more we learn about the actual science of DNA and its supporting systems, the more untenable evolution from nonliving to living and from unicellular life to human life becomes, at least for anyone who wants to apply common sense and logic.

For instance, did you know that the same strand of DNA can be read in up to six different ways for different purposes?[v] Try writing a piece of computer code that can be read forward and backward and still make sense. Then try to read that same piece of code at at irregular intervals in small pieces both forward and backward to perform different functions.[1] For DNA that works really well, but not so much for human computer programming. Now try plugging in a computer and, without any initial setup, let it program itself randomly without any human intervention and see if you can get that kind of code.

Here is what Dr. Robert Carter, with a PhD in Marine Biology, says about the flexibility of "overlapping DNA and RNA codes."

> *"Multiple, overlapping DNA and RNA codes defy naturalistic explanation and make it impossible for natural selection to operate*

---

as an agent of long term evolutionary change. Selection runs into 'a wall of insurmountable difficulty' when faced with mutations that affect more than one trait simultaneously... How could a simple process of trial and error, always seeking the simplest answer to an environmental problem, create an interleaved and multilayered system of regulation? In fact, this system is one of the wonders of the universe. Without this level of multitasking, the genome would have to be much larger and it might not be possible for DNA-based, multicellular organisms to exist at all without it." Evolution's Achilles' Heels, pp. 64-65

DNA can only do its work when the "technology" to support it is already in place. It must be created from surrounding materials, coded intelligently, and already have access to machinery to turn the instructions into proteins or to control other protein-driven processes.

I have had basic electronics repair training and computer programming training. I did not do either of those as a career, but I did find ways to apply the programming training at work in a media corporation. For example, I wrote a program to generate a report about how many times we aired a promotional ad for any cultural organization we were sponsoring. The colleague I wrote it for would enter its title or number, the start date and the end date. The program would find the appropriate logs for the dates, search them for the string of characters, find the associated time and type the text in a Word document. When it finished all of the logs within the dates, it would stop.

In order to set it up I had to negotiate with the IT department to receive permissions to go to the part of the network with the logs. In order to receive permission I had to promise to copy each log so that the original would not accidentally be destroyed or altered, then delete my copies to retain corporate confidentiality. I had to add these processes to the program and show it to the IT specialists. Every cell has an equivalent system to control access and ensure its data is not corrupted.

The computer I did the programming on and the one my colleague used it on were developed by designers and engineers in another country. It was likely built in a high-tech factory in yet another country. The language I programmed in was developed by software engineers working for Microsoft. I had to learn that particular language from the "help" files in a preexisting "macro" language in Microsoft Word.

The network I was on and needed permissions for was installed and operated by the company's Information Technology crew and consisted of servers and wiring that had to be installed and maintained by them. All of that ran on electricity provided by our provincial utility corporation from a combination of coal-fired, hydro and nuclear plants operated by engineers and technicians from all over the province.

All of these parts had to exist before I could create my small and very basic program. The point of all of this is that DNA cannot even work unless all of the parts of the cell are already in place and functioning optimally. Enzymes and protein construction machinery need to understand the "language" of the DNA code in order to know what to make and how to make it.

Enzymes and other proteins are required to "read" the code. Manufacturing machinery must be in place and working to produce the enzymes that can read the code. The machinery to duplicate the instructions (messenger RNA) must be in place to program the machinery that manufactures the proteins. Proteins and a transportation system must be in place to take the mRNA instructions to the manufacturing machinery, etc. The cell is incredibly complex. Darwin had no idea how complex this whole system within the cell is.

And it only gets worse. Multi-celled organisms produce chemicals that signal other cells to do things cooperatively with them, called hormones. Brain and nerve cells send electrical signals to other cells, too, coordinating in humans for thinking or motion or speech. How this happens is still a mystery under investigation by scientists. The "language" encoded in DNA allows all of this to happen, but how did our cells learn to "read" this language? This is also a mystery.

As I write this we are two years into a "pandemic" into which a seemingly miraculous "vaccine" (actually a genetic therapy) was introduced. It took about 30 years of meticulous scientific research and careful planning by American and European scientists to patent the messenger RNA delivery system and a team of Canadian researchers to develop the lipid nanoparticle "envelope" to protect the mRNA and allow entry to cells. Without the previous 30 years of thinking and researching it would not have been possible to develop a "vaccine" in less than a year.

Even with all the careful planning, we are discovering that this "vaccine" is resulting in unexpected effects, such as distribution of the mRNA to all major organs when it was literally designed to remain in the injection site.[vi] The production of spike protein was cleverly designed to remain attached to the cell wall of the affected cell, yet somehow managed to emerge into the bloodstream and circulate throughout the body.[vii][viii]

While some speculate that the spike protein is dangerous in its own right, my purpose here is not to speculate on safety or efficacy of this intervention. My goal is to demonstrate that the intelligence required to design the body's genetic and associated systems clearly exceeds that of even the best human researchers in our time. Our genetic systems are so finely tuned that any human interventions seem to lead to unintended consequences.

These are the things that can and do happen when intelligence is carefully applied to complex genetic systems. And yet we somehow want to believe that random mutation can produce the complex and interconnected systems that are found in all earthly organisms. Something very akin to blind faith in evolution is involved in this kind of thinking.

The findings above suggests that whoever "programmed" DNA and set up the systems supporting it is a lot smarter and "technologically" advanced than any human being. I say that this kind of amazing feat of engineering and production is worthy of a true God.

Of course, let us not forget common sense. When was the last time you saw something coming from nothing that was not a magician's sleight-of-hand?

When was the last time you saw a house or a car improve itself without help from a human being? No, there are established laws that say that energy tends to work its way down to its least usable form (entropy). Simply put, things decay or wind down. Rocks and land erode, stars burn out, and non-living chemicals have never been shown to spontaneously form living organisms because they break down in conditions of oxygen, water and solar radiation.

Why is nonsense being taken seriously by people who claim to be using the scientific method? The answer: many of them do not want to answer to a Creator God or have been hoodwinked by an anti-God propaganda campaign that tells a story about a creation without a creator.

As an example of how far this anti-God bias can go, Francis Crick, the co-discoverer of the structure of DNA, understood too well the difficulties of its formation by chance. Because he was a staunch atheist he proposed a solution: directed panspermia. In his book, *Life Itself*, he suggests that life was somehow planted on earth by advanced aliens. This is absurd pseudoscience. Evolution of life from non-living chemicals would have had to overcome the same laws of physics and chemistry on any planet as it would here on earth.

Okay, enough said about this particular subject. I may not have a science degree, but I do pay attention to what actual scientists say, and, just as importantly, what most do not say. What I mean is that there are many scientific *observations* that theories of evolutionary origins of the universe and of life do not and cannot account for. I pay as much attention to these supposed "anomalies" as I do the other observations that are used to promote the theories.

For me, the biblical account of creation week makes far more sense than the speculations of a man who classified life according to man-made imagination. This means that God created the heavens and the earth exactly the way the Bible describes Him as creating. Call me whatever you want. I stand by that statement.

The Bible has been described in many ways. Some call it a holy book. Others call it a collection of myths. It is actually a collection of historical stories, poems, songs, wisdom sayings, laws, and letters. These were written over a period of about 1500 years and gathered together into what we Christians call the Bible about 1700 years ago.

In our enlightened scientific age there is a great deal of criticism of ancient historical records, and certainly a great deal of skepticism about the supernatural. Many modern people demand a degree of scientific proof about miracles that would be better served examining the idea of cosmological and biological evolution. Real skepticism can be applied in the opposite direction, too.

One criticism that I am most fond of is, "The Bible was written by men." What book *wasn't* written by humans? *On the Origin of the Species* by Charles Darwin and *Philosophiae Naturalis Principia Mathematica* by Isaac Newton were both written by men. Why the skepticism about the Bible solely because it was written by men?

Shouldn't we instead examine each book on its own merits?

Does its message make sense? Does it seem to accord with the reality that we see around us? Is it designed to be read literally or figuratively? Is it intended as fiction or non-fiction? These are considerations when trying to evaluate someone's writing. There are many ways to write a book and many things that a book can be trying to convey.

In Newton's case it is easy to perform experiments to determine whether his conclusions seem reasonable. Those experiments have been done and Newton makes sense until you get into relativistic or quantum frames of reference. In those realms Einstein, Bohr, Schroedinger and others make more sense. Science just seems to roll that way.

Speaking of Schoedinger and Bohr, you may hear pop science talk about a lack of cause and effect or "quantum flux" in quantum physics. This can be a way of trying to explain that a universe could somehow randomly spontaneously come into being. However, just because you cannot know the precise state of subatomic particles at a given time, you cannot assume that cause and effect have no meaning.

All that the Heisenberg Uncertainty Principle means is that what you want to measure is too small for any conceivable tools to measure it with. Our tools interfere with what we want to measure because they change the state they are trying to measure. The only way to deal with systems you can't measure directly is with statistical probabilities. That, in a nutshell, is quantum physics.

Even if you could demonstrate that there is an indeterminate cause/effect relationship in the quantum realm, it would not inevitably mean that there is no God. Creating order out of chaos appears to be a well-established prerogative of God. One could more easily imagine an intelligence bringing order to indeterminacy than random chance (which, by nature, seems chaotic in itself).

Is the Bible Unscientific?

The charge that the Bible is unscientific is probably the most common one. It is certainly true that the Bible makes certain claims about how the universe and this planet came into being that are *currently* disavowed by many scientists. Six days to create an entire universe seems like a very short time to make a universe the size of the one we witness in the heavens. It gets worse: earth takes three days to form, but the sun, moon, stars and galaxies all happen on day four. That seems like quite the leap if you don't want to believe in an all-powerful and all-knowing God who created it all.

Most of the miracles in the Bible were written about by eyewitnesses or people who interviewed eyewitnesses. In no case does any of the writers claim a "scientific" explanation. They simply report what has been seen or experienced.

In fact, there is a record of one case of a man born blind who has been given sight by Jesus Himself. John, an eyewitness, in chapter 9 of his gospel, chronicles his story and the response of the skeptics.

As an aside, there have been modern advancements in the treatment of some kinds of blindness. In each case of a lifetime of blindness, restored vision almost causes a nervous breakdown due to the overwhelming flood of visual stimuli. The mind has to completely reorient the sensory system to process vision.

For a man to instantly go from a lifetime of blindness to full visual processing and recognition without being completely overwhelmed is a truly remarkable claim. This time it is the *religious authorities* who refuse to believe his story. They call him to explain what happened. They keep asking him and order him to stop lying, then accuse Jesus of being a sinner who could not possibly perform miracles. He tells them, "Whether he [Jesus] is a sinner or not, I do not know. One thing I do know. I was blind but now I see."

After some time the formerly blind man gets tired of the same questions and asks if they want to become Jesus' disciples, too. They begin insulting him and blaspheming Jesus. The man retorts, "Nobody has ever heard of opening the eyes of a man born blind. If this man were not from God, he could do nothing." The authorities throw him out of the religious establishment, of course. Even after a lengthy interrogation and shunning by the religious establishment, he sticks to his story.

It should not be surprising that secular academics do not believe in miracles if even the religious authorities of Jesus' time also didn't want to believe. The reason they didn't want to believe was that they did not want Jesus (as God!) to interfere with their authority. To me, that seems very close to the main reason for atheists not to believe in God as Creator. They might find that God demands respect and a change in how they live.

Speaking of eyewitness testimony, where are the eyewitnesses to cosmological or biological evolution? I am tempted to ask if any of those atheistic scientists was actually there to witness the formation of the universe or of this planet. What you will usually find is that assumptions about origins are based on a mindset that has already accepted evolution as its starting point, and that the apparent advanced age of our planet is based on a desire to add enough time for evolution to be plausible.

What could happen if skepticism were applied to the evolutionary assumptions about the age of the earth and the universe? One of the things you could do is test the assumptions about the radiometric dating of rocks.

The scientists at Creation Ministries International tested volcanic rocks that formed within recent history. Their results are listed in their book, *Evolution's Achilles Heels.* [ix] I posted a brief synopsis on my blog, wascanafellowship.wordpress.com.[x]

> *"When it comes to scientific circumstantial evidence the true kicker for me [is] in the case of radiometric dating. That should conclusively prove the age of rocks and fossils, shouldn't it?*
>
> *Creation ministries tried to see how accurate dating by radioactivity in the rocks is by sending samples of volcanic rock from the Mount St. Helen's volcano in 1984 and several from Mt. Ngauruhoe in New Zealand that erupted in 1949, 1954 and 1975. In a bit of a dirty trick, they sent the samples to an ordinary lab that routinely does dating for "real" scientists, but did not tell them the origin. None of the rocks had been formed before 1949.*
>
> *The youngest age measured "scientifically" in the New Zealand samples was less than 270,000 years, with other techniques yielding a range of up to 3.5 billion years. I suppose that "less than 270,000" years is technically correct, but it sure makes me wonder how accurate the technique is. The Mt. St. Helen's rocks measured at between 340,000 years and 2.8 billion years, depending on the technique used.*

The opposite problem occurs with carbon dating of coal. Using coal samples from the US Department of energy that were variously dated between 37 million and 318 million years old, scientists used a Carbon14 test. The thing about C14 is that it decays very fast compared to Uranium and other radioactive substances. In theory you can't detect any C14 after about 90,000 years. Surprisingly, they found enough C14 to date the coal to an average of 45-60,000 years.[xi] (Now there are other problems with C14 that I will go into here, but suffice it to say that the millions of years are impossible to sustain.)

So we have young rocks that are less than 80 years old that test up to 3.5 billion years old, and coal that is supposedly 37-317 million years old measuring only tens of thousands of years old. How *scientific* are radioactive dating methods, actually? Not very accurate at all, it seems. They are all based on assumptions that cannot be verified because we lack the ability to travel in time to measure how much of each radioactive material and how much of the assumed breakdown product were in the rock or coal when it formed.

In other words, there is a great deal of guesswork involved in dating rocks and organic matter. Those scientists who want the evolution theory to be true can make whatever assumptions they want to give evolution the time they think it would take.

Let's examine Carbon 14 in more detail. Carbon 14 is presently found in a certain proportion with regular carbon (as carbon dioxide) in the atmosphere. Assuming that the ratio has been constant over the last 100 million years or so, we should be able to detect the age of any organic matter that died less than about 90,000 years ago. This is based on the assumption that the amount of C14 created by solar radiation striking nitrogen atoms in the upper atmosphere is the same as the amount degraded by nuclear breakdown at any given time. The *current* ratio has been scientifically tested and is correct.

Earth is supposed to be very old, and life has supposedly existed for hundreds of millions of years. If that were the case, there should eventually have been an equilibrium in the ratio of C14 to C12 (the normal carbon we know and love) between land and sea. As it turns out, marine organisms consistently show a lower level of C14 in their bodies than found in land animals of the same age.

There are a couple of possible explanations for this. 1) The marine animals all died a long time ago and are somehow still active as zombies, or 2) the

C14 level in the oceans has not yet reached equilibrium with that of the atmosphere.

Joking about zombie marine life aside, scientists have even established a **correction factor** to standardize the ages of marine organisms with those of land animals. You can find it at: www.radiocarbon.com/marine-reservoir-effect.htm. This provides yet another clue that the earth is not as old as it is supposed to be.

Let's do a thought-experiment about carbon 14 formation in the upper atmosphere. What if the universe was created a mere six-to-ten thousand years ago? At creation, no carbon 14 has been generated by solar radiation yet, so the process begins. It takes time for C14 to be formed from nitrogen, then more time to circulate downward into the lower atmosphere. Plants begin taking up the minute amounts into their photosynthetic apparatus, and are eventually eaten by animals.

It takes even more time for the waters of the sea to take up appreciable amounts of C14, and by today it is still lagging behind the atmospheric concentration, making sea life appear older than land life, until scientists noticed the difference and accounted for it.

Anything that died within the first thousand years would have so little C14 that it would test as very old using the assumptions noted above, perhaps as old as 90 thousand years old. Some samples may not even have enough to register, making them seem even older.

The closer we come to our modern age, the closer to accurate the age "measurement" would be. I believe that this thought-experiment explains the big-picture results the "long-age earth" scientists have been cataloging as well as anything they have conjectured so far. I should point out that others long before me have conducted this thought-experiment and have reached similar conclusions.[xii]

So, how old is the earth, really? It would sure help if we could get clarification about how things actually were at the time life began on earth.

If only there was somebody who was there at the time and witnessed the formation of the earth and its life…

Oh, right, Somebody actually told us that He was there and even created it all. but we are not allowed to believe in Him.

The Bible records a meeting between the One who announces Himself as God and an audience of slightly over 1.2 million adults, plus their multitudinous children at a place called Mount Sinai, which the Bible locates in modern Saudi Arabia. (You saw that right. I will go into more detail about Sinai when discussing Moses.) In the 20th chapter of Exodus God claims, *in His own words*, to have made everything in six days before resting on the seventh. Did they believe Him? I suspect so, because Jewish people have been resting on the sabbath, the seventh day, ever since.

Strangely enough we find Jesus' disciple John claiming that Jesus was also there at the time everything was created, but under a different name, the Word. You can find that in the first chapter of John's eyewitness Gospel account. John goes on to claim that not only was the Word there, but that he did the actual world-building on behalf of His Father (John 1:1-15, 29-31) .

Who am I to automatically dismiss the claims of the only eyewitnesses to the events? For that matter, why would "scientists" *automatically dismiss, without even examining*, an eyewitness account? It seems as though the court of science only wants to see one side of the evidence.

Historical Accuracy of the Bible?

Can we increase confidence in the Bible by demonstrating that the rest of the history contained in the Bible accurate? Biblical archaeology is discovering a great deal of evidence about events mentioned in the Bible, and much of that evidence is even available on the internet. J. Warner Wallace has collected a lot of information from many sources and you can find it easily on his coldcasechristianity.com website.[xiii] Each new discovery seems to point in the direction of biblical accuracy.

As one example, many skeptics believe that Jesus Christ was not even a real historical person but was made up by the disciples or people later on. J. Warner Wallace has an article that lists several non-Christian historical documents that name Jesus and describe what his disciples believed about him. There are even letters and documents written by his opponents. *These opponents never deny that He existed*, they just did not want to follow Him and opposed his teaching.

As I looked at those kinds of evidence I could not help but come to the conclusion that the writers of the Bible knew things about the events of their time and did their best to convey them accurately in their writings. I contrast that with modern-day scholars who were not even there trying to disprove the claims of eyewitness testimony without bothering to assess the reliability of the witnesses.

As a consequence, I have come to believe that events described as miraculous are precisely that. They defy laws of science because laws of science are meant to *describe* ***repeatable*** *phenomena* that have definable causes and follow with definable effects. Science cannot account for an almighty God who created matter and energy, space and time, and who can manipulate them at will.

Who is in charge, the law or the Lawmaker? To me the answer is obvious. To me, one who created the laws of physics *obviously* operates outside of those laws, otherwise He could not have created them in the first place. If this seems like a tautology (assuming the conclusion in the initial proposition) you are absolutely correct. The difference is not only that I openly acknowledge that, but that this logic also follows everyday experience in science. Effect follows cause.

One final word about the veracity of the Bible. I have already mentioned that the books and letters, etc. were written over a period of about 1500 or so years. Many of the later writers quote earlier writers or make allusions to the words of earlier writers. In other words, they cites each other's work. As you become familiar with the Bible, these begin to jump out at you, because it happens *a lot.*[xiv] The statement I make about that may come as a shock to you, so I hope you are sitting down.

All of the citations within the Bible and the fact that it has heen studied and analyzed by millions of Jewish and Christian scholars over thousands of years demonstrate that ***the Bible is one of the most peer-reviewed works of all time***.

Add to that the fact that the books of the Old Testament were officially brought together into an approved list by the official religious authorities of the Jewish community. Add to that the the books of the New Testament were also gathered and approved by the official Christian religious authorities. Even more interesting is that the Christian religious authorities recognized the "canon" of the Jewish Old Testament writings and incorporated it in its entirety into the Christian faith.

I don't believe you can get more peer-reviewed than that.

2

What is the Bible?

There are more books in Roman Catholic Bibles than in Protestant Bibles. The important thing to note is that Protestants and Catholics agree on what books are inspired by God. The Catholic Church brought other writings from between the Old and New Testaments as well as some post-New Testament writings into their collection for purposes of studying the historical and literary background of the New Testament. In other words, the extra books are not part of the canon of the Bible, but may be useful to get a sense of the world the biblical writers lived in.

My own concerns deal primarily with the Bible as agreed upon by both mainstream Catholic and Protestant believers, so I am less concerned about studying the extra non-canonical books.

The Bible is the collected records of historians, prophets, poets, song-writers, and sages who had encounters with God or thought hard about who God is or how He works. Some recorded the history of how God worked with and among His people. Others wrote poems and songs in praise of Him, or to ask for help and/or guidance from Him. Some recorded prayers of repentance. Others recorded prayers of disappointment in God for various reasons.

Some of them even recorded things that God told them to tell the people, and thereby came to be called "prophets." Among those were some that even recorded things that God told them would happen in their future and in future generations. We call those prophecies, and many see that not a few came to pass in the person and work of Jesus Christ.

In short, the Bible contains what seems like almost every possible human response to the presence and work of the God of Israel and His Son Jesus. That is why I don't mind that the writings of the Bible were written by human beings. Only human beings can record their own reactions to God.

Since I am a Christian I am writing this book from an unapologetically Christian perspective.

What Kind of Writing is in the Bible?

What kinds of literature make up the books of the Bible? Literature professors usually use the word "genre" to frame discussions of what types of literature are involved in their studies. We might think in terms of "western" or "mystery" or "horror" as genres of modern novels. We can usually identify the difference between poetry and biography or history as we read a given passage of text in English. Believe it or not, my university English 100 class was the key to my understanding that the Bible contains a great many different genres of writing, and how to understand the way they convey information.

We can begin to identify types of writing or genres in the Bible according to some categories that we already understand. The basic ones are poetry, song, and narratives, such as history or biography. In the Bible you will also find genealogies (lists of ancestors or descendants), censuses and even a surprising amount of rudimentary financial or resource-based accounting.

Scholars have also discussed the books according to historical categories, such as the Jewish categories of Law, Prophets and Wisdom Writings. Even Jesus uses those categories when he tells the multitudes that he has not come to abolish the Law or the Prophets in his Sermon on the Mount (Matthew 25:17).

I will digress for a moment to explain how to find passages in the Bible. Much later in the history of the Bible a Jewish Rabbi named Nathan divided the Hebrew Scriptures (Old Testament) into chapters and verses in AD 1448. Christian scholar Robert Stephanus copied the system for the Latin translation of the New Testament in 1555. English versions have been using that system since 1557. So the reference above means that the passage about not abolishing the Law or the Prophets is in the book of Matthew, the 25th chapter and the 17th verse. We can shorten that to Matthew 25:17. There are many useful Bible tools online and many of them make searching by key words or chapter and verse numbers easy.

Okay, back to classifying books. The books of the Hebrew Scriptures or Old Testament of the Bible are generally grouped according to certain standard classifications. Here is the list of books by classification.

1. The Law
   a) Genesis
   b) Exodus
   c) Leviticus
   d) Numbers
   e) Deuteronomy

2. The Prophets
   a) The Former Prophets
      i. Joshua
      ii. Judges
      iii. 1 & 2 Samuel
      iv. 1 & 2 Kings

   b) The Major Prophets
      i. Isaiah
      ii. Jeremiah
      iii. Ezekiel

   c) The Minor Prophets
      i. Hosea
      ii. Joel
      iii. Amos
      iv. Obadiah
      v. Jonah

vi. Micah
vii. Nahum
viii. Habakkuk
ix. Zephaniah
x. Haggai
xi. Zechariah
xii. Malachi

3. The Writings
   a) Psalms
   b) Proverbs
   c) Job
   d) Song of Songs (or Song of Solomon)
   e) Ruth
   f) Lamentations
   g) Ecclesiastes
   h) Esther
   i) Daniel
   j) Ezra
   k) Nehemiah
   l) 1 & 2 Chronicles

The New Testament

The New Testament has three main classifications, called Gospels, Acts, and Epistles (letters). Among the letters is one that is often given its own genre: Apocalypse or Revelation. I will come back to that last one later, since its dual classification suggests that there is not necessarily only one genre within each book. A really good book to spell out most of what you need to know about genre is *How to Read the Bible for All Its Worth* by Gordon Fee and Douglas Stuart.

1. The Gospels
    a) Matthew
    b) Mark
    c) Luke
    d) John

2. The Acts of the Apostles

3. The Epistles (Letters)
    a) Romans
    b) 1 & 2 Corinthians
    c) Galatians
    d) Ephesians
    e) Philippians
    f) Colossians
    g) 1 & 2 Thessalonians
    h) 1 & 2 Timothy
    i) Titus
    j) Philemon
    k) Hebrews
    l) James
    m) 1 & 2 Peter
    n) 1, 2 & 3 John
    o) Jude
    p) Revelation (Apocalypse)

The Gospels

I will start with the New Testament books, since in some ways they are simpler in terms of genre. The Gospels are basically biographies of Jesus Christ. They differ somewhat from modern biographies in that they do not attempt or claim to describe Jesus in unbiased terms. In fact, John goes so far as to say that the events he describes are intended to create belief in "Jesus Christ, the Son of God, and that believing you may have life in his name" (John 20:30-31 New Revised Standard Version).

Don't expect a critique of Jesus or his miraculous career in these books. Unlike modern media, their bias is demonstrated for all to see. I consider that a refreshingly honest approach, but to each his own. Matthew and John write from an eyewitness viewpoint, since they were directly called by Jesus and became an integral part of his twelve disciples. John became a member of Jesus' inner circle with Peter and James, so was one of Jesus' closest confidants. His insights are unique among the Gospel writers, and he includes events and theological reflections that are not mentioned by the other three Gospels. The example of Jesus being called "The Word" at the start of John's Gospel is one such insight.

Matthew, Mark and Luke all offer similar (though not identical) windows into the life and ministry of Jesus. According to the prejudices of the Jews at the time, Matthew the tax collector was the least likely member to be invited into Jesus' band. He was a member of the hated class that overburdened the Jews to provide revenue to the Roman occupiers and who usually enriched themselves by extorting extra money from the people. Somehow Jesus was able to integrate him into a diverse group that changed the world.

Mark, called John Mark in Acts, was the nephew of an early disciple called Joseph, who became known as Barnabas (Colossians 4:10). This same Barnabas was instrumental in recruiting Saul of Tarsus (Paul) to head a mission to preach Jesus Christ throughout the Gentile world. Mark travels initially with Paul and Barnabas, but turns back to Jerusalem and is rejected by Paul for further journeys until Paul calls for him again (2 Timothy 4:11).

Mark seems to have interviewed Barnabas, Paul and Peter and probably Matthew about Jesus' early ministry in order to compile his Gospel about Jesus. I say "probably Matthew" because of the similarity in language and stories between those two Gospels. However, I am in the minority because the consensus among scholars is that Matthew relies on Mark because Mark's Gospel is shorter. Considering that Matthew was an eyewitness and Mark apparently wasn't I suspect that Matthew influenced Mark rather than the other way around. However, these scholars are all much smarter and much more erudite (scholarly) than me, so I won't be upset if you choose to side with them.

Luke, a physician who travelled with the Apostle Paul for most of his missionary journeys. has an interesting take on Jesus' life. He notes that "many have undertaken to compile a narrative of the things which have been accomplished among us." He tells us that his account comes from the eyewitness testimony others have given him, and that he sees his role as presenting it all in an orderly fashion. His is the most complete biography of Jesus, as it includes Jesus' trip to Jerusalem as an early teen, confounding the Priests at the Temple with his scriptural knowledge and wisdom. After describing Jesus' death, resurrection and ascension into heaven, he continues the story with Jesus' disciples and their disciples in the book of Acts. Luke is the only Gospel writer who bridges the story between Jesus and the ones who continued after Jesus' departure to heaven.

Within the Gospels there can be different genres. For instance, Matthew starts his Gospel with the very Jewish custom of listing Jesus' genealogy. This is a list of ancestors of Jesus from Abraham, the father of the Israelite people, through David the king who was promised an eternal dynasty. This sets him up to be hailed as the King of Israel as he is triumphantly marched into Jerusalem just before he is killed on a cross.

Luke also provides a genealogy of Jesus in chapter 4. One of the criticisms of the Bible is that they differ after David, taking different directions to get to Jesus' grandfather, of whom two different ones are listed. The key is that both Joseph and Mary are descendants of David, through different sons of David. Joseph's line goes through Solomon, while Mary's goes through Nathan. In other words, Heli was actually *Mary's* father, so therefore Joseph's father-in-law. In a patriarchal society, it was important to list him as a descendant of David and Jesus as his "firstborn" (even if by adoption).

It is also from Matthew's and Luke's Gospels that the most popular aspects of the commonly understood Christmas story are derived. Only Matthew describes the arrival of the Magi from the East. Only Matthew tells us of Herod's attempt to kill Jesus by destroying all children 2 years old and under in Bethlehem. Luke describes the appearance of the angel Gabriel to Mary to tell her that she would supernaturally give birth to the Messiah of Israel.

Luke also adds the story of the prophet and prophetess who greet the baby and offer prophetic words that Mary keeps in her heart.

Yet another genre breaks into Luke's account of Mary's reaction to the announcement. She suddenly breaks into the Hebrew equivalent of poetry in her "My soul magnifies the Lord" speech (Luke 1:46-55). Most English translations show the text of that kind of poetry in stanza-like formatting so you can tell it is a different style from normal speech. This kind of ecstatic sudden poetic expression is a surprisingly common feature of what is considered "prophecy" in the Old Testament, and you will see it often there in the Prophets and the Psalms. Just as in our own language, Hebrew and Greek poetry uses imagery and other forms of comparison, such as simile and metaphor to convey truth in non-literal ways. There are differences in how poetic lines are set up in other cultures, but the use of imagery and comparison are common features of poetry in many of them.

Obviously I have not covered everything you need to know about the Gospels in the above. I just wanted to demonstrate some of the types of literature you can expect in the Gospels, such as biography, genealogy, and poetry/prophecy. Genealogy and poetry/prophecy should be pretty easy to distinguish from biography, but distinguishing poetry from prophecy can be considerably trickier, as prophecy often takes the form of poetry or even song.

The Acts of the Apostles

The book of Acts is mostly straightforward historical narrative with the occasional visions, prophetic utterances, miraculous events, conversion stories, shipwreck and the voice of God thrown in for good measure. Greek audiences would not have been unfamiliar with any of those elements in their histories, especially those familiar with Homer's *Iliad* and *Odyssey*. In spite of my light treatment in the first sentence in this paragraph I am convinced that the events listed in Acts really happened. Luke seems to have been a meticulous historian, though his bias in favour of Jesus is certainly clear. Luke also frequently accompanied the Apostle Paul on his journeys as his personal physician, so his take on Paul's ministry is mostly from firsthand experience.

The Apostle Paul is introduced in Acts 8 and 9 as a persecutor of the Christians, and one of their fiercest opponents, even gaining Jewish government sanction to arrest Christians and drag them for judgment to Jerusalem. He is literally knocked to the ground by God and made blind. A disciple is sent to him by the voice of God and Paul converts to Jesus. Paul's story takes on more and more of the focus as the book proceeds, taking Paul from remote Palestine to the very courts of the Emperor of Rome, preaching the good news about Jesus Christ wherever he goes, whether free or under arrest.

In other words, the book of Acts is about how the good news about Jesus Christ spread from Jerusalem to the ends of the known world.

The Epistles

The Epistles are generally letters encouraging or warning Christians to remain faithful to Jesus Christ. Some are addressed to a specific church or churches, while others are addressed to specific people, such as Titus or Timothy (you can usually tell by the title).

Like modern letters, there is usually an introductory greeting, the name or names of the addressees, the body of the letter, and a closing salutation. In biblical letters there are usually instructions, encouragements, and sometimes correction to people's attitudes or actions. The body often closes with something called a "doxology," a section unique to ancient letters that describes the glory of God and may confer a blessing upon the reader or listeners. (Letters to a church were read out loud to the congregation.)

They are generally classed as being by Paul or by others, such as Peter, John, James or Jude. James and Jude were both sons of Jesus' mother Mary and her husband Joseph. They figure among Jesus' siblings and knew him the best as they grew up together.

It should come as no surprise that the letters written by the Apostle Paul make up the bulk of the collected letters from apostles and their converts. Paul spent a lot of his ministry establishing churches throughout the Roman Empire and seems to have stayed in touch with them through letters that he wrote. Thirteen of the twenty collected letters are attributed to Paul by tradition, though some modern scholars doubt Paul's authorship of a few of them.

Paul: 13 letters - Romans to Philemon

Paul spends much of his letters teaching about God's grace through Jesus Christ's mission and accomplishments. Paul's letters also establish or underlie much of the theology of the Christian church. Paul, as no other writer, describes how Jesus' death and resurrection atone for (make up for) the sins of all mankind and bring new life to those who believe in Jesus as their Saviour and King. Paul also spends time in letters to Titus and Timothy to train them in ministry and remind them of their responsibilities to their congregations.

Hebrews: one letter by a mystery author

One letter that had originally been thought to have been by Paul is the letter called Hebrews. There are many theories about who actually wrote it or to what church or churches it may have been addressed. Many of the themes in it have the texture of Paul's theology, but not the language that we would have expected from Paul. What seems most likely is that one of Paul's disciples may have written it, and it seems to come from a very Jewish perspective.

In form Hebrews is actually more of a written sermon than a letter, and it is certainly the most sermon-like in intent. Although it covers many themes of the Israelite Tabernacle and worship and compares it to Jesus' priestly function as a "Melchizedek Priest" the sermon is actually built around the event of the refusal of Israelites to enter the Promised Land after the twelve spies give their report, as found in Numbers 13 and 14. He compares our Christian walk to the Promised Land with theirs and tells us not to make the same mistake of believing the enemy is more powerful than God, then giving up before receiving the promise.

James: one letter

Some time after the death of Jesus' original disciple James the son of Alphaeus, James the half-brother of Jesus came to be a foremost leader of the church in Jerusalem, which in certain ways was considered the "headquarters" of the movement. The first council of the fledgling church takes place there as described in both Paul's letter to the Galatians (chapter 2) and Acts 15. In Acts we find James acting as chairman to proclaim the result: Gentile converts to Christianity do not need to be circumcised. This is the James who writes the letter, which clearly is intended for a Jewish Christian audience.

James' main priority is to get Christians to stop fighting among themselves and to stop being obsessed with status or class. James does not want them to let the love of wealth and status get between brothers and sisters in the faith. He calls on Christians to "resist the devil, and he will flee from you." He also corrects a common misunderstanding of the writings of his colleague Paul. Some thought that Paul's teaching about grace meant that they could sin without consequence, or had no responsibility to do good works to help others. To correct that misunderstanding James declares, "show me your faith without works and I will show you my faith by my works" and "faith without works is dead."

Jude: one letter

Jude, otherwise known as Jesus' half-brother Judas in the Gospels, has a less illustrious career, but nonetheless carries enough weight to be taken seriously by those Jewish Christians to whom he writes. Jude warns them to "contend earnestly for the faith once delivered." He seems to be noticing a watering down of Jesus' teaching among churches.

Peter: two letters

Peter writes two letters to mostly Jewish Christian converts, and even puts in a good word for his colleague Paul, whom he claims to have exceptional wisdom in his proclamation of the gospel. Most scholars believe his letters are addressed to the church in Rome, because by then "Babylon" was a well-known Christian code-word for Rome and its dissolute yet militaristic proclivities. This code-word also appears in John's last letter, Revelation or Apocalypse.

John: 3 letters and an Apocalypse (actually a 4th letter)

John becomes the second-most prolific letter-writer after Paul, and is the only writer that we know of who also wrote a Gospel. His letters are intended to warn Christians that heretical (incorrect and destructive) teachers are infiltrating the churches. That theme even carries into the Revelation's 2nd and 3rd chapters, which describe conditions in seven churches in southern Asia Minor and suggests remedies to some of them. In spite of the warnings none of those churches exist today in modern Turkey.

Apocalypse or Revelation

What many find fascinating and frightening about the Apocalypse is the many, sometimes terrifying, visions contained in it. The phenomenon is unique to Jewish literature and deserves some study. Many prophets in the Old Testament received visions from God. Some were intended to provide analogies to conditions in Israel. Some were intended to show what was literally going on behind the scenes in Israelite society, such as pagan worship at God's own Temple. Other visions were intended to show God's glory transcending time and location, such as Ezekiel's vision of God's mobile throne being carried away from Jerusalem by cherubim as a sign that God's blessing had left that nation.

Two prophets in particular, Daniel (Old Testament) and John (New Testament) had visions of catastrophic events caused by strange creatures or visions of strange creatures surrounding and/or defending God's majestic throne room. These visions often had end-times themes of overarching judgment by God, who pours out horrendous plagues on the nations or depicts rising nations such as Babylon, Greece and Persia as huge, ferocious animals with unusual features, such as wings on a lion (Chaldea/Babylon) or a winged leopard (Graeco-Maceconia) or bear raised up higher on one side than the other (Medo-Persia).

Visions like this gave rise to a genre that has been called apocalypse or apocalyptic, after the Greek title given to John's final letter. That Greek word means "revelation' or "unveiling." The discovery of the Dead Sea Scrolls has unearthed other forms of apocalyptic writings from between the Testaments. They all tend to contrast what is going on on earth with what is really going on in heaven, to show that we only see part of the picture that God sees from his divine vantage point.

In Revelation John gathers these images from the Old Testament prophets and combines them into one huge, powerful beast with 7 heads and 10 horns, representing all that is evil about the preceding kingdoms. This beast represents an end-time, world-dominating power-bloc that brings catastrophic war on mankind, and must be stopped by none other that Jesus Christ, the Son of God, before mankind becomes extinct. This is heavy stuff for the reader, but the end result is a world that looks a lot like the Garden of Eden, spread over the entire globe. John writes this to warn the church of his day and later to beware of giving up on Christ in the face of persecution and even death. The reward comes in the resurrection.

The Old Testament

As one could expect from an anthology of works written over a period of approximately 600 years, there is a lot of diversity of writing styles and genres of writing contained in what we Christians call the Old Testament (and what Jews call the Scriptures or *Tanach*). I have mentioned the three main categories above, but each book in each category may have multiple genres or styles or types of writing in it, and it is important to understand how they work to read them properly.

The Law

Genesis

Moses the Prophet is the man responsible for writing the first five books of the Bible. In some ways, calling them the *Torah* or "The Law" is a bit if a misnomer. For instance, the first book that we call Genesis is mostly a collection of stories about the ancient history of the branch of humanity that led to the nation of Israel. I have no doubt that he compiles it based both on revelations from God and on histories passed down through the generations and recorded by Egyptian scribes, Israelite family stories and Moses' father-in-law, Reuel/Jethro, the Priest of Midian.

That history begins with God, who first has to create a place fit for human habitation, the earth. God's creation of humankind is intended to benefit the rest of the created order by placing human males and females, *both* created *in God's own image,* as the dominant life-form on earth. As will be detailed later in this book, events in the garden that God plants in Eden set the course of human action and morality in a downward spiral that leads God to intervene at different points to preserve a remnant of people that He works with in various ways through history.

The story-flow of the book is enhanced in places by genres such as genealogies or visions or poetry. Genealogies are there to connect the characters to the history of their ancestors through the flow of time. The poetry is usually indicative of a very human response to events of a miraculous or hoped-for outcome. Visions or verbal communications from God are fairly commonplace in Genesis and suggest that God communicates with humans when He desires to do so. Most of what we need to know about God comes from His communication with human beings. Science may provide some, though not all, clues to the "how," but only the Creator God can supply the "why."

The main takeaway from Genesis is that God establishes covenants (agreements with rights and obligations on both sides) with various people throughout the book. These covenants lead to a promise to Abraham to create a nation from his descendants. This nation would be in a special relationship with God the Creator. God promises that he would deliver Abraham's descendants from slavery after about 400 years. This covenant will also eventually lead to a blessing on all the peoples of the world through Abraham's "seed" or offspring. Whether that "seed" is one person or many is not specified, but becomes clear much, much later.

Exodus

In Exodus the extended family of Israel finds itself in a condition of harsh slavery, including an intentional genocide (a situation not unfamiliar to the Jewish people even in modern times). God allows a "miracle baby," Moses, to survive and be raised in the royal household of the Supreme Ruler, the Pharaoh. Moses learns both Egyptian ways and the ways of his ancestors, and eventually makes a murderous choice, leading to his self-imposed exile from Egypt. In Midian he meets and marries the daughter of Reuel (also known as Jethro), the priest of Midian. He becomes a shepherd working for his father-in-law.

40 years later, God encounters Moses at Mount Horeb (Sinai) and chooses him to be his spokesman as He delivers Israel from slavery with intense plagues and mighty miracles. God destroys Egypt as an economic and military power in the process. After leading them miraculously through the Red Sea to Mount Sinai in Arabia, God establishes a covenant with the nation, complete with laws they must obey to remain in God's good graces. He will provide blessings for obedience and curses for disobedience.

This book contains what may be the lyrics to first recorded song in the Bible, a worshipful response to their deliverance from Egypt through the Red Sea (Exodus 15:1-21). That passage also refers to the first person named as a prophet, Moses' *sister* Miriam. This may help us remember that God made both man and woman in His image. (We later learn, of course, that Moses is also a prophet, the most important in Israel's history.)

It is at the point of making a covenant with Israel that the component of "law" seems to come to the forefront in the Bible. Initially the covenant is comprised of chapters 20-23, which is the legal code that God literally inscribes on the two tablets of stone that is most often associated with the Ten Commandments. After Israel sins with an idol of a golden calf, the law is expanded upon and a Tabernacle with ritual sacrifices is set up to atone for sin in Israel. Between legal sections there are accounts of Moses meeting God as well as exhortations to obey God's commands in order for blessings to follow.

Leviticus

Moses compiles God's commands for the priesthood of Aaron and his descendants as well as the entire priestly tribe of Levi in the book now called Leviticus. Most of the book is a record of God telling Moses what to tell the priests or the people about how to sacrifice the offerings made to God for various purposes, such as sin offerings or fellowship offerings.

Other parts of the book are stories about what happens when the Tabernacle is finished and the priesthood is set apart as holy to God. There is even a story that warns about what happens when a priest disobeys the instructions (Leviticus 10). (Important safety tip for priests: follow the instructions *very* carefully. You don't want to be "fired" by God.)

Numbers

The book now called Numbers is called that because it features censuses, taken at the start and end of the journey from Sinai to the Promised Land, some 40 years later. The first few chapters detail the preparations for departure to the promised land, while the rest follows Israel's trek through the wilderness and the reason for the 40-year trip that should have taken only a few weeks at most: disobedience.

The short story is that Israel refused to enter the Promised Land, so God cursed them to wander for 40 years until all the adults who refused died in the wilderness. With the exception of Joshua and Caleb, who trusted God and wanted to enter the land, only those less than 20 years old at the time of the refusal would be allowed to enter. The second census was taken to confirm that all those who had been adults at the refusal (with two exceptions) had died.

Deuteronomy

This book gets its name from the Greek words for "second law" due to its major emphasis on providing rules for Israel to follow once in the Promised Land. The book is mostly comprised of Moses' last speeches to the gathered people of Israel before they cross the Jordan River to enter the Promised Land.

Within this book Moses makes various prophetic predictions that Israel will fail to keep its promises to God and therefore be "vomited out" of the land of Israel. They would be scattered around the world, persecuted and never knowing lasting peace until a prophet like Moses arises among them to deliver them back to God and to the inheritance promised to Abraham. Moses even writes and performs a song that poetically reminds them of their future failure and restoration in chapter 32:1-45.

The book concludes with the appointment of Joshua, who would lead them into the Promised Land and the death of Moses on Mount Nebo, within sight of the land that he would not enter. I won't spoil your reading by telling you why Moses was not allowed to enter.

Some scholars claim that Moses could not have written Deuteronomy because he obviously could not have recorded his own death. It is clear that the description of his death was obviously written by someone else, probably Joshua his assistant and successor as leader of Israel. This does not prevent him from having written everything else attributed to him. The fact that Jesus seemed comfortable assigning the Law to Moses makes me comfortable with that, too (Matt 19:3-12, compare with Deuteronomy 24:1).

Everything else in the Bible relies on the accounts in these first five books to set the expectation of the redemption of Israel from its future enslavement. They will be liberated by a Moses-like Prophet who will also draw people from all nations into God's embrace because of the promises God made to Eve and to Abraham in Genesis.

The Prophets

Historical/Biographical Books

The Prophets are a broad category of books that tell the story of Israel's rise and fall. The story is told in narrative, poetry, song and very brief biographies that tell only barest details you need to know about various heroes and opponents of God's will for Israel.

Certain books emphasize the narrative of Israel's rise, such as Joshua, which details the initial conquest of Canaan by Israelite forces. A period of instability is chronicled in Judges. 1 & 2 Samuel highlight the progressive unification of Israel's tribes under a central authority under Samuel, then Israel's first king Saul, and finally the hero-king David. Ruth, a love story, is a brief biography that shows how even a dispossessed non-Israelite widow can become part of the royal line leading to King David.

From the peak of Israel's power and status among the nations, 1 & 2 Kings follow the dynasty of David to the eventual disintegration of Israel and its destruction as a political unit through bad leadership and internal division, leading to Assyrian and Babylonian domination and the end of the nation as a political unit. What remains of Israel is carried off to captivity to Chaldea as slaves to the Babylonians. Although 1 and 2 Chronicles are classified as "writings" rather than "prophets," they follow a similar trajectory, but rather from the perspective of priests and prophets attached to the Temple in Jerusalem.

In English Bibles Daniel follows Ezekiel among the Prophetic books, even though the book of Daniel is considered a Wisdom book and is classified among the Writings, I include it here because it has historical and biographical elements within it. For instance, Daniel is an eyewitness to the last night of Babylon's independence.

Daniel is a Judean prince who becomes a captive in Babylon and rises to become a leading advisor and regional administrator to King Nebuchadnezzar. His career spans the height and destruction of the Babylonian Empire, whereupon he rises in the courts of the Medo-Persian

Empire due to his integrity and wisdom, eventually becoming once again a valued advisor and regional administrator.

Both early and late in his career he receives visions from God about how the powers of the world will be defeated by none other than God Himself at an appointed time. Daniel is even given a timeline of 70 "sevens" of years until God sends a Deliverer - a Messiah - to the remnant of Israel in Judea. This Messiah would end up dying, but yet somehow deliver His people at a later time. Daniel apparently lives to see Ezra lead a small remnant back to Jerusalem after their 70 years of captivity.

The book of Esther. Some time after Daniel's death a young Jewish orphan woman Esther is dragged into King Artaxerxes' harem after the king divorces his wife and sends her off to exile. The king is looking for a new primary wife, and young Esther is the most compelling in her beauty and demeanor, so she becomes queen. The book never mentions God, but does show how fragile Jewish life under Gentile rule is, exactly as Moses predicted. Haman, a royal courtier from a particularly nasty branch of the family of Esau persuades the king to order the genocide of the Jewish people. Esther must put her life on the line by exposing herself as a Jew to save her people. Haman's schemes are turned back on him and the Jews are saved... this time.

The books of Ezra and Nehemiah follow the work of Ezra the Scribe and Nehemiah the Governor as they return a small remnant of Judah to resettle Jerusalem and its environs under the rule of Persian kings. Ezra returns to re-establish the worship of God by rebuilding the altar and eventually rebuilding the Temple, though with only a shadow of its former glory. Nehemiah arrives to work later and rebuilds the walls of the city, making it somewhat defensible against its many enemies once again. As Daniel predicted, the city would be established during times of trouble, and so trouble would continue for centuries.

Prophetic/Poetic/Visionary Books I: The Major Prophets

Daniel has two contemporaries as prophets, Jeremiah and Ezekiel, whose works are prominent in the prophetic literature. However, before discussing them we must begin with the earlier prophet to whom they owe a great deal, Isaiah.

Isaiah

Isaiah is referred to frequently in the books of 2 Kings and 2 Chronicles in connection with reigns of some of the few righteous kings of Judah. The ten tribes of northern Israel had split from Judah and Jerusalem as well as the dynasty of David several generations before and Isaiah ministered to warn them of the impending collapse of northern Israel to the Assyrian Empire. He served under four generations of Judean kings before being tortured and killed by Manasseh, Hezekiah's rogue son and successor.

His book is comprised mainly of statements that God makes for him to tell the kings of Israel and Judah. That is interrupted by the story of Isaiah's induction into the role of prophet as he sees a vision of God on His throne with his entourage of cherubim. He makes Isaiah clean by touching a burning coal to his lips and sends him to prophesy about the destruction of Israel and Judah if they do not turn back to God. Things got better for three generations of kings in Judah, but Israel did not listen and was destroyed during Isaiah's ministry while Hezekiah reigned in Judah, the southern part of Israel. (There will be more detail about the split between the northern and southern parts of Israel later in this book.)

Isaiah also contains a number of memorable poetic passages, some of which have been incorporated into Georg Handel's famous oratorio *Messiah,* such as "for unto us a child is born / unto us a son is given…"(Isaiah 9:6-7) and the "he was despised and rejected…" passage from Isaiah 53. The rest of that chapter goes on to describe how this messianic figure both dies for the sins of the people and comes back to rule. That passage comes as no surprise for Christians, but leaves ancient and modern Jews scratching their heads. Imagine that! A servant of God who dies for his people, but comes back to "share the spoil with the mighty." Strange indeed!

Jeremiah

Most of Jeremiah's book is comprised of direct quotes from God to Jeremiah, which he is to pass on to the people and rulers of Judah.

Jeremiah has a tough job. He gets to remind Judah that God is not happy with their performance and will soon bring their kingdom to an end. This bad news is unsurprisingly not well received by the corrupt kings of Judah. David's legacy has greatly degenerated, leading Judah into Babylonian vassalage and eventually the demise of the nation. Jeremiah has the dubious privilege of being proven correct about the will of God. In the process he takes up many of the themes of Isaiah and even of Moses about how the people of God will be scattered and maligned among the nations, even though a small remnant will be preserved during the hard times.

Like Isaiah, however, he also looks forward to better times in "the day of the Lord." There will be a new covenant (Jeremiah 31:31-35) that includes having God's law written "on their hearts" and that God will "forgive their wickedness and remember their sins no more." He promises that God will allow them to return to their land after the 70 years that Babylon will rule the world. This promise becomes the trigger point for Daniel's "70 sevens" prophecy about the Messiah. Jerusalem is resettled and rebuilt after 70 years, but the Messiah doesn't show up for 483 years after that. There will be more about the Messiah later.

Prophetic/Poetic/Visionary Books 2: The Minor Prophets

The books categorized as "Minor" Prophets are called that only because they are much shorter than those of the "Major" Prophets. Four of the books were written during the time of Israel's divided kingdom. The northern part, the "house of Israel, had an uneasy relationship with the southern "house of Judah." Hosea, Amos and Micah were written to warn the northern kingdom that God was not pleased with their religious, moral and political decline. They do so in various and very interesting ways.

Jonah tells the story of the most successful prophet of Israel in turning a nation around: Israel's enemy Assyria. It is ironic that Jonah was displeased with God over his success at turning Assyria from their sinning ways. He apparently felt that God made him a traitor to his own people. God reminds him that Assyrians are people, too, and also need redemption.

The next four books (in order of when they were written), Nahum, Habakkuk, Zephaniah and Obadiah, were written after the house of Israel had been destroyed by Assyria. The prophets are now mobilized to warn the house of Judah not to fall into the same wandering away from their God that destroyed their northern kin. Some wrote before Jerusalem fell, while others wrote after the majority were slaves in Chaldea (Neo-Babylonian Empire).

The final four books written, Joel, Haggai, Zechariah and Malachi, were written during the time Persia ruled over what had been Babylon. Most of them were warning the remaining Jews to repent and return to God so that God would resettle them in their land, or, once returned to their land, that God would prosper them if they obeyed His commands.

Hosea

Hosea wrote after Isaiah, and God spoke to the house of Israel by using Hosea's married life as a sign to Israel. It was a tough assignment, as Hosea was commanded to marry an unfaithful woman who lived the life of a prostitute. This lifestyle was how God characterized his relationship with Israel, the wandering prostitute. Hosea loves her, but she is virtually impossible to live with. So it is with God and Israel.

Jonah

The story of Jonah and the giant fish is one of the most well-known biblical stories that can be greatly misunderstood. Jonah tries to escape the mission God sends him on to warn Nineveh, the capital of the vicious Assyrian Empire. They have been judged by God and will be utterly destroyed. Assyria is in the east, so he heads ***west*** by ship and ends up thrown overboard. Swallowed by a giant sea creature, he survives for three days inside it and is "vomited" onto a beach. He reluctantly completes the mission and is disappointed that the Ninevites repent and are spared. He finishes by complaining to God that God is being too merciful to Israel's enemy, which was why he did not want to warn them. The point is that Gentile nations sometimes repent when they fear God's judgment, but Israel does not.

Amos

Amos prophesies in a way that reminds us of prosecutors bringing charges of breaking the criminal law. God judges Israel according to the covenant's regulations, but also judges the surrounding nations for violating the territorial integrity of their neighbors. Joel uses the poetic imagery of locusts devouring the land to describe the desolation that will follow a refusal of the house of Israel to repent. There are even what looks like court proceedings as the prosecution presents its case against the nation.

Micah

Like Isaiah, Micah prophesied during the time Assyria was taking over the northern house of Israel. The language in a lot of this book sounds like a lawsuit against the house of Israel and pictures a courtroom setting. God is filing a lawsuit based on the covenant, which will not be broken entirely even if they are judged guilty. They will experience the curses and will be redeemed according to the promise.

Obadiah

After the siege and destruction of Jerusalem, Obadiah speaks God's word about God's judgment on the nation of Edom, the traditional adversary of Israel. Edom assisted Babylonian forces in taking over the southern kingdom's capital and occupied much of its land until well into the Persian takeover of the area. Obadiah prophesies Edom's judgment at God's hand and the restoration of Israel and Judah.

Nahum

Just in case you were wondering if Nineveh completely escapes God's judgment, read the book of Nahum. It looks like the following generations forgot Jonah's story and returned to evil aggression against its neighbors, including the house of Israel and even well into Judah, even besieging Jerusalem until it was supernaturally delivered. (That is a story in itself! You can read that in 2 Kings 19.) Nahum uses the language of God going to war against Nineveh and wiping it out as a nation.

Habakkuk

Habakkuk is written as a conversation between the prophet and God. The prophet asks God why there is so much evil in the nation, but is shocked at the means by which God plans to intervene. How can God use a nation even more evil to destroy the evil in his own nation? When he complains about that to God, God responds by saying that every evil nation will get its turn to be judged, and that God is and will be the final Judge who makes all things right. The last chapter is a song in response to God's answer.

Zephaniah

Zephaniah's "book" is actually one extended song, as evidenced by the accompaniment on stringed instruments (the 8th century B.C. equivalent of guitars and harps). The movements start with universal judgment of the whole earth and moves to God's judgment of specific nations, ending with Jerusalem's fall and restoration "at that time."

Joel

Joel begins with the analogy of locusts devouring all the crops of Israel to describe the devastation that will occur to the house of Judah if they do not repent. The nation will be totally destroyed, with nothing left in the land if they do not turn back to God. The final chapter describes the woes God will inflict on the nations that abuse the Israelite people He allows to fall into their hands. The lesson: God judges not only his own people, but also those who deal with the descendants of Abraham. He blesses those who bless them and curses those who curse them.

Haggai

Once a small group of settlers leaves the Babylonian exile to return to Jerusalem and environs with Ezra under Persian rule, problems begin with neighboring provinces. They had been commissioned by King Cyrus to return to Jerusalem and rebuild God's Temple, but had not been doing that work. Haggai is told to speak to the people and ask them why they think God might not be blessing them the way they had hoped. The answer: God gave them a job and they weren't doing it. He also tells them not to be disappointed in how shabby the new Temple looks compared to the magnificence of the old one. When God is there it has enough glory.

Zechariah

Zechariah writes in support of the work of Nehemiah, who is temporarily governor of Judea. Nehemiah is commissioned to fortify the city of Jerusalem from its enemies. Zechariah is given dozens of prophetic visions to strengthen the will of the inhabitants and give them hope of a future restoration to the fullness of Israel as a kingdom under a strong Warrior-Messiah. Israel will be so popular that people will come to worship its God by participating in the Feast of Tabernacles, though some reluctant adversaries might have to be more forcefully persuaded to attend than others.

Malachi

In Malachi God takes on both sides of a conversation with the returnees of Judah, accusing them of certain specific violations of the covenant and voicing their dismissive response with the formula, "in what way have we…[done that?]" He then goes on to answer with specific charges. Malachi ends with a hope of redemption of the righteous and a reminder to remember Moses' law. He predicts that an "Elijah" will come to Israel before "the great and terrible Day of the Lord.

The Writings

This section of the Bible is often referred to by scholars as the books of wisdom. They can contain song, poetry, discourses, conversations, short proverbs, and narratives. that are told for purposes of describing the reality behind our perceptions of the world and how it works. Wisdom in the Bible is not just about figuring out knowledge or about how things work. Wisdom is also about how to live fruitfully in a manner consistent with God's revelation about who He is and about what His will is on both a global and individual scale.

Job

The book of Job is the story of a wealthy, God-fearing man to whom the unthinkable happens. He literally loses everything: possessions, children, even his health. The story is mostly about his reaction and that of three of his long-time friends to his misfortune. What is unusual is that we get a look under the hood of his trials in the very first two chapters. God is challenged by a "satan" (think of a prosecuting attorney) in his royal court. The challenge is that Job will give up on God if he loses all of his blessings and begins to suffer unjustly. God accepts the challenge - and the rest is history. There are long discourses about justice and guilt among Job and his friends, and a meeting with God Himself at the end. I won't spoil the ending if you haven't read it yet.

Psalms

The book of Psalms is basically Israel's book of hymns. They cover a range of topics, from prophetic utterances to meditations on God's character dealing with human injustice, disappointment with God, restoration of trust in God, repentance and restoration with God, pleas for help and thanks for deliverance. It seems as though every possible human response to God can be found in the songs of Israel.

Proverbs

Throughout history national leaders have surrounded themselves with the advisors whom they considered to be the wisest or most technically competent in the realm. How do you train the next generation of critical thinkers? Give them a cross-section of deep sayings that make them think. The book of proverbs is the Bible's version of what many cultures have tried to inculcate in their leading officials. The book begins with a long discourse by Solomon about the need for wisdom, then goes on to warn against various ways that people lose out on their best life, health and wealth. The book then provides many deep short sayings that make the reader think about how to live a worthwhile life and how to manage themselves and others to best advantage.

Ecclesiastes

This book is often dismissed as a book that talks about how meaningless life is. This is where genre becomes important to understand what it is conveying. Archaeologists have discovered a class of books they call "royal autobiographies" in several Ancient Near Eastern texts. This refers to books written by kings to impart important wisdom to their heirs to guide them to making good decisions. I suspect from internal evidence that Ecclesiastes was written by or for King Hezekiah, who is described as somewhat more righteous than David and possibly wiser than Solomon (at least he does not seem to have more than one wife). Unlike Solomon, Hezekiah never wanders from God, which seems consistent with the conclusion of the book, "fear God and keep his commandments, for this is the whole duty (or "wholeness") of man."

The vanity or meaninglessness comes from neglecting to enjoy the journey while you make a living. What is the point of working yourself to death for wealth if you don't enjoy what you have already earned and share it with good companionship, especially within a happy marriage?

Many scholars have missed this point by claiming that he is arguing against the wisdom found in Proverbs. Not so. Success is good. Just *don't spoil success by neglecting to enjoy it while it lasts*, because for many reasons you cannot control, it may not last forever. A song you might recognize captured this spirit when the writer sang, "…so have a good time. The sun can't shine every day."

Song of Songs

I like to characterize this song as "the ballad of the one that got away." This seems to be a song based on the story of a young woman who is locked away in Solomon's harem while pining for the love of her life, a poor shepherd. She escapes and they run off together and enjoy each other's love. If you are sexually inexperienced, be prepared to blush. Because of the sexually explicit material many commentators have tried to downplay the sensuality by making it an analogy of Christ and the church. Read it for yourself to see if that is the first thing that comes to *your* mind.

Daniel

Considered a book written by a wise man, Daniel is a collection of history, biography and visionary literature, making it hard to categorize. Daniel has prophetic visions, yet started as a Jewish prince taken captive as a young man. Somewhat like Joseph in Genesis, Daniel is given the ability to interpret dreams and thereby comes to the notice of King Nebuchadnezzar, who promotes him to ever-more important positions. Daniel's wisdom keeps him head and shoulders above his contemporaries and even earns him the esteem of God Himself, who then sends the angelic messenger Gabriel to inform him of what is to come by means of interpretations of his visions and of interpretations of statements by Jeremiah. Not many stories in the Bible are more well-known that that of Daniel in the lion's den.

The Importance of Genre

How the Bible says things is important in understanding *what* it means. Reading a song lyric that calls a woman's neck "a tower" doesn't mean that she has a long and powerful neck. It actually means that she stands tall and proud, and is probably not impressed by your advances. Expressions like "at his right hand" refer to divine approval and authority granted by God to rule on His behalf.

You can get a sense of the difference between narrative and poetic in the two descriptions of the death of the Egyptian army at the crossing of Israel of the Red Sea. The narrative in Exodus 14:27-28 describes the Lord as allowing the sea to go back into its place, drowning the army. In Exodus 15:21 Miriam describes it as "both horse and rider he has hurled into the sea." "Hurled into" give the impression that God took them from land and threw them in, but that is just poetry to highlight the fact that God *actively* destroyed the army by drowning them in the waters that returned to their natural place.

Descriptions of strange creatures coming from out of the earth represent things other than Godzilla-like sci-fi creatures, but rather an evil empire, such as Babylon or Rome. A "mountain" or "hill" in the right poetic context can mean a nation or government, and so can a tree or bush or vine or even a vineyard.

You also need to read beyond just a small part of a passage to get the full meaning. Reading Job's defense of his integrity does not mean that Job is being "self-righteous" as many commentators have charged. Remember that *God* is the one who claims he is "blameless and upright." As character references go, that is pretty much the best you can get. Something else is going on in what is happening to Job, and you have to dig to find it. The digging is where a lot of the fun is.

Let us see where careful reading takes us as we explore what the Bible says about how this world started.

3

Origins

I have already told you that I was a science geek in high school and had already dismissed the bizarre notion of biological evolution of species by Grade 9. Yes, I know that natural selection is scientifically established. How else do we have so many breeds of dogs and cattle? My contention is that they still remain dogs and cattle, and reproduce, in biblical terminology, "after their kind."

All around us we observe what happens to objects and even landscapes over time. They get older and decay. Nowhere do we ever see improvements in anything without intelligent intervention. Any theory that requires constant spontaneous improvements in highly complex systems flies against every scientific experiment ever made. You might be able to make a gooey tar with some poisonous amino acids out of lightning and ammonia/methane in an atmosphere[xv], but only if you game the system by creating a special chemical trap and cooling vat.[xvi] However, you certainly won't make DNA or a functioning cell out of it.[xvii]

What about the origin of the earth, moon, planets and stars?

Genesis 1 tells the story of the making of the entire cosmos by the Creator God.

He seems to start by making water, of all things. Then He creates light, and separates it from darkness, starting the day/night cycle. (This is before creating the sun.) He calls the first iteration of day and night "day one."

On the second day God separates waters into "above" and "below" with a space in between. We will see on day four that the "space" in between is big enough to accommodate all of the stars and galaxies in the universe, translating what God calls it as "sky" is completely inadequate. A corollary seems to be that this story places the earth at the center of the universe.

Modern science has its own strange ideas about Christianity and its supposedly superstitious literal interpretation of the Bible. As an illustration, the common story passed down to us from scientists is that Galileo was a brave scientist who found a truth that the church declared as heretical: the idea that the earth moved around the sun and was therefore not at the center of the universe.

First of all, the Bible does not specifically teach about whether the earth is at the center of the solar system, though it does imply that its location is at roughly the center of the universe. Do you see the difference? The universe is vast almost beyond imagination, and the distance between the earth and the sun is minute compared to the apparently 13 or so billion light-years of its radius. Earth may well be at the center of the universe, since we see no difference in numbers of stars or galaxies in any direction we point our telescopes.

A little-known fact about the Galileo controversy in the church is that the church's official doctrine about the earth-centered universe had been adopted from Aristotle, a pagan Greek philosopher, who taught and wrote in the early to mid-300's BC. Re-discovery of Aristotle's works helped energize the Medieval church and helped set up modern science during the Renaissance. (Strangely enough, Muslims had been sitting on this information for centuries before this Western "rediscovery" and had not done much with it.)

Don't get me wrong. Aristotle was a brilliant man who put that brilliant mind to work studying the world around him. His work on logic was still being taught in the CEGEP college I attended in Quebec. I can still tell the difference between syllogistic reasoning and weaker inductive reasoning, thanks to Aristotle and my Humanities 101 professor.

Aristotle had rightly reasoned that if the earth revolved around the sun, it should be possible to measure the degree of parallax to one of the nearby stars from different points along its orbit to see a difference in the angle. That of course was a brilliant piece of induction that turned out to be correct. That is exactly the method later used to measure the distance from earth to nearby stars.

When measured by Aristotle and others up to and beyond Galileo's time there was no measurable difference in the angle, so Aristotle assumed that the earth did not revolve around the sun. Unfortunately, the precision measurement tools to discern planetary motion around the sun did not exist in either Aristotle's or Galileo's days, a span of about 1600 years.

The distance is so great to even the closest stars that the tiny degree difference could not be discerned until after Galileo's death, when better instruments were invented. Without being able to provide evidence beyond mathematical theory, Galileo could not convince the Pope, a scientist who was actually initially on his side, to change the doctrine.

There were mistakes on both sides of the Galileo story. The church's mistake with Galileo was not a hidebound reliance on the Bible for its doctrine. The mistake was confusing Aristotle's take on earth's central place in the solar system with Bible truth about earth's place in the universe. In other words, the church trusted a pagan scientist to help them create church doctrine.

Galileo's mistake was to try to publish as truth what he could not yet prove empirically. Put those mistakes together and you can find the real story of Galileo's "heresy." Without proof, the church could not stand behind his theory. Trying to publish it as fact rather than as theory in church scientific papers without empirical evidence is what made it heresy in the eyes of the church.

Putting the entire blame on the church is a mistake, as is any other form of historical revisionism. The church trusted an outsider's science and the insider did not have the evidence needed to overturn the scientific consensus of the day.

The reason I tell this story is twofold. First, scientific consensus is always supposed to be challenged by independent thinkers with new and sometimes better theories. This means that calling any scientific consensus as "settled" is almost always premature. Second, the history of science, like many other histories, can become self-serving and self-obsessed. By making the story of Galileo a "science versus religion" story with Galileo as the hero, we forget the human beings and the real issues on both sides of the story. The conflict is actually about science versus science, with Galileo versus Aristotle and Ptolemy. The church simply chose one side of the debate over the other instead of staying with the Bible and observing what it says and what it does not say.

There has never been any reason to believe that the Bible teaches that the earth is at the center of the solar system, though it might well be at approximately the center of the observable universe, give or take about 93 million miles.

On the third day God makes the ground "appear" and gathers the waters into "one place." This suggests a single landmass surrounded by seas, but hey, what would the Bible know about the ancient supercontinent of Pangea? God also claims to have "brought forth" all of the land plants, including seed-bearing plants and fruit-bearing trees on that day.

On the fourth day God creates the sun, the moon and all the stars. The way it is written, the stars are almost an afterthought, quickly dispatched into the heavens on a divine whim. The sun, moon and stars are there to mark times, seasons and sacred festivals, *even before humans arrive*. This suggests that humanity, far from being a randomly evolved being, was actually the plan all along. As suggested earlier, the space between the "waters below" and the "waters above" is said to be large enough to accommodate the sun, moon and stars.

This is followed on the fifth day by waters "bringing forth" fish and other sea creatures. On this day the birds and flying reptiles and flying mammals are also created. And they all reproduce according to their kinds.

On the sixth day the land "brings forth" land animals and other creatures. Notice that each of these sea and land creatures reproduces "according to its kind." That is the origin of the biological definition of a "species." Each kind of animal can adapt to a certain degree to its circumstances but can only reproduce within its own kind. This is what Gregor Johann Mendel discovered in his experiments. This is also what science has yet to disprove by natural observation. (This is not to say we cannot mess around with genes in the lab to produce hybrid creatures. It just doesn't happen in nature by natural laws.)

Finally, God completes his creation by creating humankind in His own image. Something changes here. God does not order the land or the water to produce these beings, but rather tells Himself to do it. He also makes sure to tell us that both man and woman are made in His image. This contradicts a great many ancient creation myths that suggest that man and woman are separate creations, even sometimes by different deities.

We are then told that *God is very pleased* with this handiwork, and *especially with the humans*, and rests on the seventh day, calling it "holy time." This is the origin of the Jewish sabbath, created within the very first week of the universe. This is also the origin of the concept of the seven-day week. The fact of a sabbath rest also highlights another basic requirement: work. What is God resting from? He is resting from His work of creation. While He does not in this particular passage create a requirement for humans to rest one day out of the week, we suspect that it will show up at some point in the human story. More on that and the implied idea of work later.

Let us pause the story here for another comment about the creation. I have already commented about why biological evolutionary hypothesis makes no sense based on findings in genetics, even going back to Gregor Mendel's work. The same can be said of the Big Bang hypothesis of cosmology. Believe it or not, several "fixes" have been required to make the hypothesis fit observed facts.

One problem that you would only find in astronomy and cosmology journals is that scientists have grave difficulty figuring out how to form stars out of expanding hydrogen and helium clouds that would have formed in the Big Bang.[xviii] The mathematics of the theoretical physics predicts that the energy required to bring the universe into being would be so great that the energy would take some time and cooling to precipitate into atoms of hydrogen and helium and little, if anything, else. It would have to become an expanding gas cloud as the excited hydrogen atoms eventually found partners to bind with into hydrogen molecules. (Helium, as an inert element, would not bind to anything and therefore remain as independent atoms.)

To grasp the problem here, try to imagine compressing air molecules without a container to put it into and you will see what I mean. When you press the release on a can of compressed air, does the uncompressed air around it enter the bottle or does the compressed air flow out of the higher pressure to the lower pressure air. Now, imagine trying to compress even lighter gasses in a vacuum into a tight enough space to create nuclear fusion. Humanity's only reliable way to induce hydrogen to fuse requires intense lasers or nuclear fission to ignite it. How do you do that in the vacuum of space?

The only viable theories about star formation require the prior existence of stars that can explode to push those gasses together. So where did the first star come from? While reluctant to mention that conundrum to the general public, cosmologists have been scratching their heads over that for decades and have no real answers.

Recently, an attempt to explain star formation has invoked "dark matter" as a gravitational source for gas compression. Get this: dark matter cannot be seen or detected by any instruments, (it emits no light or other radiation) but must somehow have a strong gravitational attraction in order to compress gasses. Hmm, an undetectable type of matter that exerts force. Unfortunately, believing is not seeing.

Here is another example. If galaxies are billions of years old the spirals in spiral galaxies should have amalgamated into discs because outer edges move at the same rate as the inner parts of the arm, but over a greater distance. Because they haven't all become discs, the fudge factor of "dark matter" had to be applied to the outside edges of galaxies in order to maintain the spirals over such long time intervals.

Of course, spiral galaxies are certainly possible if they have *not* been around for billions of years or have started spinning recently. That could mean the universe is as young as God claims it to be. Oh, right, I can see those scientists in the back row fidgeting, so I had better move on.

It gets worse. The universe's expansion is said to be accelerating through no force that we yet understand. We now have to invent "dark energy" to keep the Big Bang hypothesis fitting the observations. According to some estimates, dark matter and dark energy comprise 94-96% of all the "stuff" of the universe.

We are expected to believe that what we see in our visual and radio telescopes is only 4-6% of the universe and the rest is stuff we will never be able to measure or see. How does that even remotely make sense?

Getting back to galaxies, the Hubble Telescope has taken Ultra Deep Field images of a section of space with no visible stars. What surprised astronomers was the number of galaxies discovered in a tiny portion of dark sky, and the apparent distances of those galaxies. Astronomers try to point to a number of odd-shaped star clusters and call them proof of early galaxy formation, but I cannot help but notice many spiral galaxy formations surrounding them. The star clusters seem like pretty ordinary formations like the globular and open star clusters much nearer our own Milky Way galaxy. If galaxies that far away look just like galaxies much nearer, they probably are roughly the same age as our own galaxies. If they are so far away that the light took billions of years to get here, why do they appear to have the same age as ours?

The most interesting and surprising thing about the Ultra Deep Field images is that, according to the Big Bang idea their apparent distance means that the light should be from a time before galaxies could possibly have formed. Why are galaxies even there, unless the theory is missing the mark?

But wait, there's more. Studies of the temperature of space indicate that the whole universe has a very even temperature. What is wrong with that? According to theory there should not have been enough time for the heat energy to dissipate across the entire 26 billion light-years of distance, so another fudge factor called "an inflationary period" had to be invented. There is no physics that can explain how this inflationary period started or stopped.[xix]

This heat problem actually is remarkably similar to the problem of how we see light from distant galaxies if the world is only 6000-ish years old, except over a greater time-scale. What if the oft-stated references to God "stretching out the heavens" in the Bible is actually what happened? That could explain the rapid expansion of the universe so that both light and heat would have travelled to be visible and evenly "warm" across the universe.

So here we have a theory that misses the mark so often that several unscientific and scientifically unverifiable "fixes" have to be applied to make it work. And even with the fixes applied, the gaps are so huge you can drive a galactic super-cluster through them. Stars that cannot form, galaxies that should not exist so early, and no physics to explain how it all started at all and where the energy to start it all came from.

A scientist might ask me, "So, smart guy, how do *you* explain all of this?"

So, why can we see light from galaxies so far (13 billion light-years) away? One possible answer: if God made it, why not? You might call that unscientific, and you would be correct. On the other hand, a hypothesis that calls for unseen matter and energy with magical properties and a physics-defying expansionary period strikes me as a pretty unscientific hypothesis too. Oh, and did I mention the impossible stars?

Those are only a few of the problems with a cosmology that tries to create a universe without the God who claims to have created it in the beginning.

What you might not be aware of is that there are four competing cosmological theories that are consistent with what the Bible teaches about the creation of the universe that have been proposed. Three Bible-believing scientists have come up with theories that rely on Einstein's General Theory of Relativity to explain how we might be able to see light from so far away in a 6000-or-so year-old universe. Two of the four were developed by Dr. Russell Humphries using different conceptions of how *actual* matter and *real* energy are applied to the fourth dimension (outside of space-time). I will mention one of the simplest as an example.

As I understand it, the first one by Dr. Humphries requires that the earth be at roughly the gravitational center of the universe. When God creates the stars and galaxies, they are all relatively close to our solar system, and the gravitational potential approaches that of a black hole at the center. This means that on day four of creation that time, as measured on earth, stops. As God stretches the universe away from our solar system the gravitational potential decreases until we pop out of the black-hole-like state, starting time again. From our perspective, the universe of stars and planets suddenly appear on day four. There was already light reaching earth, from the formerly close stellar objects, so light shifts toward the red end of the spectrum as the stars are moved away in the stretching of space-time.[2]

I will digress for a moment about an unrelated but still pertinent item about creation and science. Dr. Humphries also devised a theory that accurately predicted the field strength of the magnetic fields of the planets of our solar system. He did this before the Voyager One and Two fly-bys of the outer solar system. When magnetic field data were sent from the probes, Humpries was closer by orders of magnitude than the magnetic dynamo theories devised by evolutionary believers. This does not mean that he is necessarily correct about the starlight problem, but it does mean that he is a deep thinker and seems to have some idea of what is going on in the universe.

---

[2] Origins: Starlight and Time. This YouTube video discusses Dr. Humpries' theory of how light reaches earth from billions of light-years away on the fourth day of creation week in an accessible way for a general audience.
https://www.bing.com/videos/search?q=russell+humphreys+youtube&&view=detail&mid=CF47146ED1114B033DDFCF47146ED1114B033DDF&rvsmid=F8421D4CA137516BC220F8421D4CA137516BC220&FORM=VDRVRV

Dr. Humphries started his magnetic field theory with the Biblical story that everything started when God created the heavens and the earth from water (Genesis 1 and 2 Peter 3:5). He reasoned that *if* the water molecules were all initially oriented in the same direction, collapsing it into planets would change the orientation of the positive and negative ends of the molecules, generating a collapsing magnetic field. Transmuting water into planets with liquid cores would allow such a magnetic field to slowly decrease its energy in a predictable pattern, which he calculated within his specialty of electro-magnetic engineering and physics. Dr. Humphries' theory also is the only one that explains why magnetic fields of all liquid-core planets measured, including earth's, are measurably declining in energy over time.

There is one more thing to note to the decay of earth's magnetic field. It demonstrates that life on earth only has a short time to be sustainable. More than about 10,000 years ago the magnetic field would have been too strong for life with nervous systems to exist, and in about 2000 years it will become too weak to keep out deadly radiation from the sun, causing mass extinction of all life on earth.

Since the man already has a successful theory based on elements of the biblical account, I believe it is worthwhile to consider the possibility that one of his two theories, or those of the other two scientists, about how we see distant starlight from about 6000 years ago might also prove successful if proper testing ever becomes possible.

I also want to remind us that the reason Christians believe God created the universe *is that* ***He tells us*** *that He did it and also gives some, though not all, details about how He did it.* In other words, Christians start with a known and move toward the unknown. From the known, we can work out possible scenarios to fill in the gaps. We can then test the scenarios against the revealed scripture and see if it makes sense. Without that starting point of revealed knowledge, secular science starts with even more gaps about origins, and fewer ways to test their assertions.

If chapter one is the story of God's creation of the overall universe, chapter two narrows it down to God's creation of the humans and their story on earth. Some claim that the story contradicts chapter one, but that one is easy to explain. We are transported to a special place on earth. This is a place that God would claim as a special portion for Himself and for humankind. At first it is a patch of desolate land in an otherwise beautiful and productive world. This will be a place where God will plant a garden, and will have the man and woman tend it for Him.

God forms a man from the soil of the ground and breathes life into him with His own breath, making the inert earth alive and conscious. He places the man in the garden. This garden is watered by a spring that feeds a river that passes through the garden. This river branches into the four main rivers that bring fresh water to the whole world. One gets the impression that this garden is on high ground at the center of the earth. This idea of a river that originates from God's garden paradise on earth is one that will be repeated in prophetic writings throughout the Bible.

God gives him instructions to guard and tend the garden and a task: to name the animals. In other words, God gives him *work* to do. Remember the sabbath day of rest that God takes? It implies that the other days of the week are for doing work. Fortunately for the lazy among us, we are not necessarily told *how much* work we must do each day.

Adam does what God asks, and begins to notice that each male animal has a complementary female, yet there is none for him. He is alone. God points out that it is not good for a man to be alone. God then sedates the man and surgically removes a rib from him, which he grows into a woman.

The science geek in me sees the logic of the scenario. Men have a pair of dissimilar chromosomes labeled X and Y by scientists. The Y chromosome is what gives men their male characteristics. Women have matching X chromosomes (X and X) this pairing is what gives them female characteristics. It makes sense for God to make the female from the male rather than the other way around. This is because He would not have any Y chromosomes to work with if He started with one woman. (This is not to say that God could not do so working from a woman. The result, however, would involve creating a being that was not quite "flesh of my flesh and bone of my bone," because a change in genetic structure from an X to a Y would be required.)

More importantly from a psychological and social standpoint, this establishes that men and women are literally made from the same "stuff," making them equal in God's eyes. **This should make men and women equal in our eyes, too.**

Men and women have a joint dominion over the earth according to God's instructions in Gen. 1:26-27. The second chapter establishes the "how" of how He does this. He does this by making them literally from the same flesh and bone. Adam acknowledges this when he sees her for the first time, claiming that she is "flesh of my flesh and bone of my bone."

This profound reality promoted by the story is ignored by those who would see women as inferior to men by the will of God. It is also ignored by those who see the Bible as a misogynistic work that promotes the domination of women by men.

Many of the pagan views around at the time of Moses claim that man and woman were made separately from each other. They also suggest that all the chaos in the world is solely as a result of the weakness of woman. Take the story of Pandora as an example. She opens the box and lets all of the evils loose on the world. In her case all that is left in the box is hope, which she lets out also. We will see how the bible treats Eve differently.

What does it tell us that "science" believes that "mitochondrial Eve" and "Y chromosome Adam" may have existed 200,000 years apart? Does that really make man and woman equal? I am just wondering...

Notice also that this biblical creation account of man and woman as genetic complements leads to a union of a man with a woman. This is the very basis of the marriage institution. A man and a woman are to become "one flesh."

This is not just a sexual union. This is a joining of mind, heart and effort. This is a mutuality of goals and desires. This is working for the common good of each other and the children that will be created by the love of the two. The "wow" turns into a "how" as the two communicate and come to mutually satisfying agreement about what to do and how to go about it.

As we look around us at marriage today, we can't help but notice that something has gone wrong. There seems to be a struggle to get along and increasing divorce. We learn the real cause of the problems between women by men in the following chapter of Genesis.

Chapter 3 of Genesis begins with what appears to be a casual conversation between the first woman and a snake. Say what??? Why is the woman talking to a snake? Better yet, *how* is the woman conversing with a snake? How is she understanding him?

Actually, this reminds me of the many aboriginal stories that tell of a time in ancient history when humans and animals talked freely with one another. It would be easy to dismiss this biblical story as myth, but I suspect that there is a reason so many cultures have stories of humans and animals talking to one another. Maybe ancient cultures knew something about early human-animal relationships that we moderns are willfully ignoring or calling mere myth.

There seems to have been a breakdown in human-animal communication at some point after Eve's conversation with the snake. (Maybe God didn't want other animals giving the humans any more big ideas?) Perhaps it had something to do with the next big biblical event: the worldwide flood. We will get to that after we discuss how a conversation with a snake changed the world.

So, back in the Garden of Eden we find man and nature in harmony. Unlike the dystopian description of "nature red in tooth and claw" that defines the evolutionary process of survival of the fittest, we find peace and life expanding over the world. Humans are fruitarian and animals are all vegetarian. Death does not mar the peace of the world. Only when God warns the man to avoid eating from the one tree God designates as off-limits does the threat of death enter the story. The "tree of the knowledge of good and evil" is a tree that God reserves to Himself alone. God warns the man that eating from it will result in the curse of death.

Enter Eve and the snake. I presume that it is not just snakes that can converse with humans at that time in history. Otherwise we might wonder why Eve does not seem startled by the serpentine conversationalist. The snake poses the question of whether God is looking out for their best interest by denying them the fruit that would "make them wise" and allow them to "be like God, knowing good and evil." This leads her to question God's motives and she reaches for the fruit and eats it.

We learn that Adam is with her and does not try to persuade her not to eat the fruit, which he also eats. We are not told how long Adam had been with her or how much of the conversation he had heard, but we do know that God had specifically told *him* not to eat of it, or he would die. Upon eating it, "their eyes were opened" and they realized that they were naked.

I have to stop here to point out something strange. The woman's eyes open only after Adam eats the fruit. Why only after Adam eats it?

We are provided with two clues in the story. First, *Adam* is told about the rule against eating the fruit *before* Eve is created from his rib. The second clue is that Eve's telling of the rule includes the idea of not even touching the fruit, which is not included in God's instruction to Adam. Adam probably added that touch to emphasize the danger when he told the woman what God instructed.

In other words, as the one who heard God personally, Adam was personally responsible to God for the obedience. Since he was with her by the time she ate the fruit, he could have tried to stop her. By not attempting to stand up for God and then adding his own disobedience, he becomes the one primarily responsible for the trouble that ensues. In 1 Corinthians 15:21 Paul says, "Since death came through a man, the resurrection of the dead comes also through a man." In a letter to Timothy, a young pastor he trained, Paul explains, "Adam was not the one deceived; it was the woman who was deceived and became a sinner."

If the woman was deceived and became a sinner, why is the man to blame for all the death in the world? Precisely because *he knew what he was doing when he ate the fruit.* He knew that what he was doing would result in death, and *he did it anyway.*

One thing that I have never seen considered by others who comment on this story is its relationship to mankind's mission in the world to "fill the earth and subdue it" and "rule over" the fish, the birds and all land-dwelling animals. They are there to be in charge of the creatures of the earth, not to be ruled by them.

This suggests to me that an important aspect of the story of Adam, Eve and the snake is a story of abdication of ruler-ship over the creation by following the snake's recommendation to disobey God. In Romans 1:25 Paul talks about how the bulk of humanity "exchanged the truth about God for a lie, and worshiped and served created things rather than the Creator." I suspect that this is how it started, with obedience to a reptile instead of the true God. Idolatry is only a small step away from obeying the creature instead of the Creator.

Once their eyes are opened, they tie fig leaves together to hide their nakedness and try to hide from God. God confronts them and asks why they did it. A blame game begins, with Eve blaming the serpent for deceiving her and Adam blaming God for giving him his wife, then blaming Eve for giving him the fruit.

God is less than amused, so he decrees that they will live according to the much harder path they set for themselves by deciding what is right and wrong for themselves. This starts the tragic path that has ended up in the world we know today, with all of its beauty marred by death and violence, chaos and the extinction of entire species of animals. In addition to those problems, the descendants of the woman will always be at odds and sometimes even be enemies with the "descendants" of the serpent. In other words, some human beings will follow God and others will follow the serpent and his minions.

There is good news within the bad, however. Adam and Eve, and all humanity thereafter will die, but not before they give birth to further generations of human beings. Eve will be the mother of all living human beings, and one of her "seed," or descendants, will deliver humanity from the results of the serpent's lies. The serpent will "bite his heel," but the "seed" will stomp on the serpent's head, destroying it.

Rather than sulking at the news, Adam realizes that they will live for a while yet and see their children grow up. He gives his wife the name Eve, because she will be the mother of all living humanity. They are given quality leather clothing. (Yes, God kills at least one animal and skins it.) They are then removed from the garden so that they no longer have access to the tree of life.

It is important to note that **the tree of life was intended to be a source of everlasting life** for the mortal humans. The *inaccessibility* of the fruit of that tree *becomes the reason they eventually die.* Later the idea of choosing life or death will revolve around the imagery of the difference between the tree of life and the tree of the knowledge of good and evil. Making the wrong choice leads to death.

It took almost a thousand years for Adam and Eve to die, but they ended up in "the dust of the earth" from which they had been taken. And so has every other human being from that point forward. Life also became harder for humans, ejected from the garden and making their living from toiling in the ground. Planting crops and milling grains was much harder work than maintaining the Garden of Eden, especially with weeds cropping up everywhere.

Family life became harder too, as the bond of trust between husband and wife was shaken by the blame-shifting, and each spouse tried to control the other. We do not know how many children they had, but somehow, as their children grow up, fraternal jealousy rears its ugly head. God honors one brother over another at a sacrifice. We are not told why God chooses one sacrifice over the other, but Cain sulks. He is chastened by God about allowing sin to rule over him when his job is to rule over himself and control his impulses. Instead of learning from God's advice he lures his brother away from their camp and kills him in a jealous rage.

The first generation born to the first man and woman now has the distinction of having the first murderer and first murder victim. Adam and Eve must have been devastated by the dual tragedy of their two sons. One dead, and the other a murderer and an outcast.

Some have wondered where Adam and Eve's children managed to find spouses, since everyone knows it is a sin to marry siblings. We are told that Eve is the mother of all human beings, so the obvious answer is that they married their sisters. It is certainly true that laws against marrying close family in modern Western culture derive from biblical laws found in Exodus, Leviticus and Deuteronomy. What is not generally understood is that those laws were not necessary when humanity started out. Adam and Eve were perfect physical specimens with a fully intact genome that had not yet started to degenerate into harmful mutations.

So yes, brothers and sisters did marry in those first few generations. There was no genetic reason not to. Remember that Adam married a woman *cloned from his own genes*, so how is marrying a sibling at that time really different? Somehow all of the genetic diversity in humanity has derived from the two genetically perfect human beings who started the whole race. It is only as the race degenerated that it became necessary to spread out the gene pool to keep bad mutations from reinforcing each other by intermarriage. Laws against marrying close family came into being only when necessary, roughly halfway through human history.

At this point it might be useful to do a thought-experiment about the evolutionary hypothesis. How did the first fully human male meet the first fully human female? Did they develop separately and against all odds manage to meet at just the right time to produce offspring? Were humans independently evolving in different places at the same time so they could eventually meet and cross breed? Or were they siblings of the same parent ape-like creatures? I don't believe those questions have ever been adequately answered in the evolutionary hypothesis. Evolution of human beings from lower life simply defies logic and common sense.

Okay, back to the storyline. God tries to prevent further murder by putting a mark on Cain, presumably to prevent someone taking vengeance on him. (Remember that every human being is a close relative and may want revenge.) God curses the ground under Cain, forcing him to find some other way to make a living. Rather than tending sheep like his deceased brother, he goes east and begins to establish cities. It is not clear how that works, but he may be creating trade centers to earn his living by providing shelter and taking a cut of traded goods.

Technology develops quickly, and we find that by generation eight, human beings are already working iron into tools and weapons. This is why a coal miner was able to find an iron hammer embedded in a chunk of coal at a site. How it got in there is quite the mystery, unless you believe the Bible about human and geological timelines. I will say more on that later.

We also find human morality degenerating at the same time as technology is improving. Cain's great-great grandson becomes the first recorded bigamist, and also kills a man, claiming it was in self-defence. Clearly violence is on the rise in human society. It then comes as no surprise that his son Tubal-Cain is the first recorded blacksmith, forging tools from bronze and iron.

Chapter 5 brings the story back to Adam and Eve, who produce another son to take Abel's place, Seth. Seth's family line is traced in an extended genealogy through to a man named Noah and his three sons, Shem, Ham and Japheth. Each generation lives several centuries, with Methuselah holding the record at 969 years. From him on, the human lifespan decreases by large increments, especially rapidly after the worldwide flood, until we get to the standard "threescore and ten" (70 years) mentioned in the Psalms.

Did they really live that long? Did the ancients not know how to count years? Other ancient chronicles also attest to extremely long lifespans early in human history, so why not? Did every ancient society exaggerate the lifetimes of their early kings? Why? Could it be that perfect human genetics combined with a strict vegetarian diet of fresh greens, grains, fruits and nuts could have been responsible? That seems likely to me.

Chapters 6-9 tell what is likely the most well-known and supposedly debunked story in the Bible: the Deluge or worldwide flood. Scientists would rather believe that Mars was once covered in water than believe that the earth was once completely submerged at any point in history. If there was never a worldwide catastrophic flood, why do mountains all around the world contain marine fossils near their peaks?

The lead-up to the flood story is quite controversial in Christian circles just in itself. A race of "sons of God" marries "daughters of men" and produce giant, prodigious offspring called Nephilim. It seems that human beings by this point are so violent and evil that God repents of making them and wants to destroy His handiwork. Is there a connection between the "giants" or Nephilim and the violence? There are extra-biblical Jewish writers who claim that the "sons of God" are actually non-human or angelic beings who intermarried with human women to produce hybrid angel-human offspring. The prime example is the Book of Enoch, which names them and describes their intent and even their geographic headquarters in the pre-flood earth. These fallen angels have not only intermarried with humans but have also taught them civilization along with war and dark magical arts.

This theory proved too much for delicate theological sensitivities of some prominent Christian and Jewish thinkers. Augustine of Hippo devised a work-around for the older "angels" interpretation, claiming that they were actually degenerate descendants of Cain who married descendants of Seth, dragging them into dissolute lifestyles. Medieval rabbis Rashi and Nachmanides preferred to think of them as despotic human rulers of all bloodlines who arrogated divine titles to themselves and forcefully took wives into their harems. In our time many UFO enthusiasts claim that the Nephilim are "ancient aliens" who once ruled the planet or brought civilization to humanity.

Peter (1 Peter 3:19-20 and 2 Peter 2:4-5) and Jude (Jude 1:6) both seem to be okay with the "angels who married women" interpretation of Genesis 6. Considering that Jude grew up with Jesus and Peter was one of his three best friends, it would be easy to suspect that Jesus would have told them if that was not the case, since He presumably was there as the Word at the time. The Word would have been the one who bound the disobedient angels in *tartarus*, the "underground prison for spirits" version of "hell." That version of hell is different from the more common *hades* or "domain of the dead" for humans that we can think of as "the grave."

Since we are told in the Bible that God created the beings that we call angels, and we are not told that God created extra-terrestrial alien beings from other planets, I will assume that the fallen angel theory is the correct one. That suggests to me that we may be looking in the wrong place for "extra-terrestrial intelligence." Rather than scanning the heavens we should be aware of the non-human intelligences that once resided in heaven and are now bound to earth and its environs, as well as those who still work around God's heavenly headquarters.

Getting back to the story, humanity has become completely evil after roughly 1650 years since Adam. The one notable exception to this is Noah, a biologically completely human person (as opposed to a hybrid human-angel being), "perfect in his generations." Noah also happens to be a God-fearing, righteously moral human being who pleases God.

God decides that the entire world needs a reset (a "reboot" in computer terms). He decides to destroy the world by flooding it with water to kill all air-breathing animals and people. Since He made the world out of water, this is the most natural solution to the problem. In poetic terms God had "set the boundaries" of the waters, and He could set them loose. God could have done that in any of several ways miraculously. We are told that God "opens the windows of heaven" and that "the fountains of the great deep were broken up."

What might cause the waters to rise above the land? You might try sinking the continents. You might try heating the oceans by several degrees to cause huge amounts of water vapor to then come down as torrential rains. Raising the ocean temperature would also cause the volume of the ocean water to increase, covering some of the coastal areas with ocean water, too. What if the "fountains of the great deep" refers not just to water, but to the liquid rock that underlies the crust of the earth?

What if the answer is "all of the above?" You might have a solution that explains how the supercontinent of "Pangea" rapidly splits into the seven continents we know and love now, along with the flood. This theory that creation-minded scientists call "catastrophic plate tectonics" even provides a scientifically reasonable mechanism for the ensuing ice age. That is, if you have warm oceans and cool land (due to massive cloud cover) you would have long winters and short summers, allowing snow to accumulate into ice sheets over a few hundred years.

Yet God has a couple of loose ends when it comes to destroying humanity. What about the promise to Eve that one of her offspring would rescue the human race from the serpent's designs? Also, what is to be done about the one righteous man and his family? Will God wipe them out, too in order to restart the world?

The conundrum is solved by involving Noah and his family in the process of restarting the world. God tells Noah to build an "ark," a barge-like, non-motorized floating zoo to carry each "kind" of air-breathing animal to safety on the other side of the flood. God promises to make a covenant with them if they will obey.

There is a lesson here about obedience. Had they disobeyed you would not be reading this. Nor is it likely that I would be writing this.

They build it and the animals come. A male and female of each of the "unclean" kinds and seven pairs of each of the "clean" kinds. The "clean" kinds are the ones that God would accept as fit for using as sacrifices. Later on these would be the kinds that God allows Israel to eat, in their intended role as a "kingdom of priests."

Now we should talk about "kinds" of animals. As mentioned in the introduction, the biological definition of a species is that animals of the same species can interbreed to produce viable offspring. In other words, their offspring are fertile and can produce young of their own. That is what a biblical "kind" refers to. What modern scientists often call different species may actually be of the same kind if they can mate and produce viable offspring. For instance, all animals in the genus *panthera* (all the large cats) can produce viable offspring with all others. Lions, tigers, panthers, cheetahs, jaguars, etc are all one kind. Only two animals could have represented the entire group aboard the ark. For instance a tiger-lion hybrid male and a female panther-cheetah hybrid could have produced all of the varieties of big cats we see today. There would have been plenty of room in the ark for all of the "kinds" of air-breathing land animals if each "kind" was minimally represented in this fashion.

Likewise all of the modern so-called "races" of humanity are all of one kind. The different skin, eye and hair colors, height differences would easily have fit in the eight human beings assigned to carry on the human race. All three of the males were Noah's own sons. The three women of presumably mixed human heritage married to them would have provided all of the variations we see today. This would also explain the singular findings that all males are descended from the same individual. This is based on the discovery that the Y chromosome in all human males shows descent from one male individual. Scientists informally call him "Y chromosome Adam." Either the biblical Adam or the biblical Noah might well have been that person.

Women, in a similar vein, are all apparently descended from one woman due to findings that the DNA in female mitochondria (the "powerhouse" of every cell) show descent from one female human. Because scientists have no imagination, they have dubbed her "mitochondrial Eve." Since the three daughters-in-law who disembarked from the ark were likely from different families, it seems most plausible that the biblical Eve was the true mitochondrial Eve. An apparent time gap between mitochondrial Eve and Y chromosome Adam might be explained by Eve and Noah respectively.

The biblical flood also explains why the current variety of animals we have is far less diverse than what is seen in the fossil record. It also explains the strange resemblance of many modern animals to others identified as separate species in fossils. Giving a fossil duck a different name than an identical modern duck does not have it cease being the same variety of duck. But wait, there's more…

When visiting the fossil dig near Eastend, Saskatchewan I could not help but notice the proximity of the dinosaur and mammal fossil beds. Of course I do not know whether they are in the same rock layer, but I did wonder why they ended up being so close.

An article in *New Scientist* (12 January 2005) points to a fossil found in China that overturned the idea that only small mammals existed in the Cretaceous period. What they found was a large mammal fossil with a smaller dinosaur inside it. This mammal had eaten the dinosaur before suddenly dying and being rapidly buried. Findings like this eventually led to other scientists seeking mammal remains from the Cretaceous period to fill in the ecological gaps.

It turns out that remains of 432 mammal species, many virtually identical to modern forms, have been found in the same layers of rock as dinosaur fossils. That is almost as many as the dinosaur species that have been found. For instance Thomas A Stidham notes in *Nature* 396, 29-30, November 5, 1998, that the data suggests that almost all modern bird groups existed alongside dinosaurs in the Cretaceous period. According to evolutionary hypothesis, large varieties of mammals and birds should have arrived much later.

Perhaps scientists who specifically study dinosaur fossils can be forgiven for not noticing the mammal fossils nearby, at least initially. Perhaps scientists who study mammal fossils can also be forgiven for not noticing nearby dinosaur fossils. Curious indeed. I suspect a Bible-sized blind spot in scientific endeavors. One has to wonder how long it takes to notice things that contradict one's world-view.

Speaking of not noticing things that contradict a worldview, here are a few fun facts, mostly taken from *Evolution's Achilles' Heels*[xx]:

1. Soft tissue has been found in dinosaur bones. In fact, non fossilized dinosaur bones have also been found. They cannot be millions of years old, unless you are a True Believer in evolution.

2. Carbon 14 dating of multiple layers of coal beds spread across the USA reveals roughly the same age of coal deposits, around 45-60,000 years. Fun fact: Carbon 14 should no longer be measurable after about 90,000 years, placing the so-called Carboniferous period much closer to our time than the 30 million to 300 million years assigned to them. This means that almost all coal formed at approximately the same time, suggesting a singular, probably worldwide event.

3. Carbon 14, has also been found in dinosaur bones and tissues. When you combine that finding with the soft tissue, you have to consider the likelihood of a demise of the animals of thousands rather than millions of years ago. When the evidence was first presented at a geophysical conference, the organizers were so upset that they removed it and all mention of it from their conference website.

4. Remember the iron hammer found in a chunk of coal? How would that get there if there were no humans around during the so-called carboniferous period? (Aliens? If they had the technology to get to earth from light-years away, one suspects they would be using something more sophisticated than iron hammers.)

5. There is no evidence that Coal is currently forming in swampy areas of the world. Why do scientists assume it must have been doing so in the past?

6. On the other hand, Coal appears to be forming in the lake near Mt. St. Helens. This is due to floating logs dislodged from surrounding hills after a landslide pushed a huge wave through the forest. The trees cover a large portion of the surface of the lake and rub against each other, knocking waterlogged bark off. The bark settles to the bottom

and is covered in sediment, creating peat. Compress the peat under sediment long enough and it turns into coal. Other coal beds show evidence of formation by compressed tree bark among sedimentary layers.[xxi]

7. That is not the only interesting phenomenon from the Mt. St. Helens explosion. The various species of trees floating in the lake above get waterlogged at different rates and settle at the bottom of the lake in different stratified layers, giving the impression of a succession of forest types. That explains what looks like a succession of forests in different rock strata.[xxii]

8. Give a rock formed from a recent volcano to a radiometric dating lab without telling them where you got it and the dating will invariably be wrong by a factor of hundreds of thousands to millions of years. This is the method used to "disprove" the young-age carbon 14 dating of dinosaur bones.

9. There are four commonly used radiometric dating isotopes used in dating rocks. Every one of them yields widely differing dates from the others when used on the same rock. Does this make you feel confident in the accuracy of the methodology? This point and the one just previous make it highly doubtful.

10. Fossilization does not take millions of years. If that were so, some discoveries would be impossible. A fossilized teddy bear, a fossilized sack of grain, and a toy car almost completely encased in stone have all been found. In addition, an experiment with wood left in a mineral hot spring found that it completely fossilized within 7 years.

The above observations do not fit into a hypothesis that fossils formed over millions of years. There are many other observations that could be included, but I believe that these will do to illustrate my point. All of the above do, however, fit into a theory that recognizes a geologically active worldwide deluge such as mentioned in the Bible. There is overwhelming evidence that the earth and its creatures have been around for a much shorter period than claimed by the evolutionary hypothesis.

So we have a worldwide flood that provides worldwide sedimentation and rapid burial of land and marine creatures of all kinds, many of which resemble modern creatures. The rapid burial allows preservation and minerals in the salty water enable fossilization of many of the buried creatures. Human civilization is wiped out, and the flood becomes the subject of traditions around the world, eventually becoming warped into legend and changed as it is told and retold for generations.

In the meantime, a group of 8 adults is safe on their amazingly engineered refuge upon the waters. They are surrounded by representatives of all the kinds of life on board their vessel. The boat is probably about 510 feet long, 85 feet wide and 51 feet tall. These dimensions ensure stability in rough waters, according to modern shipbuilding standards. It is good to point out that of all flood stories in the world, only the biblical one has a ship with dimensions that prevent it from capsizing in storms. The biblical Noah was a much better engineer than the Sumerian version, Utnapishtim, who built a large cubical box as a boat.[xxiii]

The waters cover the earth for roughly a year and the ark eventually settles on a mountain in the region of Ararat. The family leaves the ark and sets the animals free. The family sacrifices some of the "clean" animals in thanks to God for their deliverance from the flood. God is pleased with them and their sacrifice, and enters a covenant with them.

There are several things to note about this "new covenant." The first is that it begins with *almost* the same command that God gave Adam and Eve, to "be fruitful and multiply and fill the earth." God wants the earth to be filled with humans, unlike certain "green" activists who think that humanity is a blight or a cancer on the earth.

A second thing to note is that the beginning with the command to be fruitful and multiply suggests that God's original assignment for Adam and Eve was also part of an earlier covenant. The basic rules of that original covenant were to get married to one person of the opposite sex, multiply, spread out over the world, rule over the planet, including all the birds, sea creatures and land creatures, eat seed-bearing fruit, and don't eat the fruit from one tree that is for God alone.

A third thing to note about the post-flood covenant is that, instead of "ruling over" all of the animals, birds and sea creatures, God tells them that all the creatures will instead fear and dread the humans, because they will now become food for humanity. (If I were an animal, I would not be pleased either.)

A fourth thing to note is that eating blood is forbidden to humans. They can kill and eat animals, but only if they bleed them out first. Of course, the first covenant was a fruitarian one, so this did not need to be included in that one. God makes it clear that blood is something that belongs to God's purview as the life-source of man and animals, and that it must be treated with respect for God. Blood becomes symbolic of life, and that conditions the rest of the covenant.

Fifth, humans are to mete out judgment upon murderers by killing them. This is a radical departure from God's treatment of Cain. Exile is no longer enough to ensure that murder is kept at bay. Deterrence now becomes the norm.

A fascinating sixth element is the inclusion of responsibilities given to animals in this covenant. Yes, animals are given instructions, too. They are not to kill human beings. Killing a human being is a God-prerogative, one that he gives to judicial human authorities, not to animals. Just in case you think I am exaggerating the idea that God includes the animals in the covenant, here below are verses 8-10 of Genesis 9. I italicized part of the passage to emphasize the point that we might otherwise miss.

> *Then God said to Noah and to his sons with him: "I now establish my covenant with you and with your descendants after you and with every living creature that was with you—the birds, the livestock and all the wild animals, all those that came out of the ark with you—every living creature on earth..." (New International Version.)*

I was shocked to realize that the covenant with Noah and his family was also a covenant between God and the animals. That says something incredibly positive about the intelligence that God gave the animals. They are capable of following God's instructions, but it is much more than just instinct. If they have to be accountable not to kill human beings, they must also have a degree of will of their own. Why would God have to threaten them with death if they disobey?

Some preachers attempt to teach that humans are better than animals because we are intelligent and animals only have instinct. They are completely wrong. Anyone who has dealt with animals, whether pets or farm animals, knows that they have individual personalities and habits. Cats, for instance, can be very manipulative of their "owners." One often wonders if the cat is truly in charge of the household in many cases. Dogs are usually well-known for their loyalty and will brave incredible dangers to protect their human owners. How can these be possible if at least some animals do not have some form of consciousness?

The point to take away from this observation is that God is even concerned about the relationship between human and animal, even in a degenerating world. He gives the animals fear of humans to protect them to a degree from human predation. He also protects humans from animals by ordering them to avoid killing humans. It is a very one-sided relationship to be sure, but it is one nonetheless. We were meant to live in the world, and tame it, not destroy it.

The fact that God considers animals to be part of His covenant should warn us against abusing them, even if we need to kill them to eat. It also should remind us that God created the ecosystem that we depend on for survival.

Unlike the revisionist narrative taught in modern and post-modern schools, Christians and Jews throughout history have understood this and have tried to live in a sustainable way. The Industrial Revolution allowed greedy entrepreneurs to undermine what had been a basic Judeo-Christian worldview of care for the environment to one of dominating nature with technology.

Noah's sons and daughters-in-law go on to found the next wave of human civilization, with their children and grandchildren beginning to spread out to retake the world. Remember that God wanted humanity to completely fill the world.

One problem begins to develop, however, when Noah's great-grandson Nimrod begins gathering people into cities that he establishes. Nimrod becomes the first post-flood empire-builder. From that beginning, the city that eventually came to be known as Babel (or "confusion") is founded, and a monumental building project is planned. The plan is to build a tower "that reaches heaven."

It is not enough that humans have now rejected God's command to spread out and multiply, but they also want to invade God's own heavenly domain. Just as many angels desired to leave their assigned heavenly roles and settle on earth, humans seem to desire to leave our earthly home to invade God's heavens.

Naturally God is concerned about the rapid technological progress that could short-circuit His longer-term plan to redeem humanity, so He intervenes by confusing the languages that the people speak. The ensuing chaos drives many to start moving away with others who understand their language. It turns out that floods are not the only tool in God's toolkit. It certainly makes one wonder what has stymied our efforts to settle on the moon for 50 years. It will be interesting to see how Elon Musk's attempt to colonize Mars turns out.

We learn from other places in the Bible that God assigns various parts of the post-flood world to the different family groupings. Since they do not seem to want to follow God, He also assigns them angelic overseers who are supposed to care for them and supervise their development. (You can see glimpses of this in Psalm 82 and Daniel 10:12-14.)

The earliest texts of the Old Testament available are found in a Greek translation commissioned about 250 years before Jesus' birth. The earliest versions that have been found have a different rendering of Deuteronomy

32:8 than is found in current versions. In verse 8, according to the older versions, Moses speaks of the time when God divided the nations at the time of Babel. When He sets up their boundaries" he sets them according to the number of the "sons of God." Later versions say "sons of Israel," which in itself is strange, since Israel does not exist as a nation until centuries later. The earlier version makes more sense, especially if you understand that "sons of God" is a reference to angelic beings that existed at the time of the formation of the earth (Job 38:4-7).

From this point in the Genesis narrative the worldview of the story narrows to the descendants of Shem. Via another genealogy, from Shem the story rapidly moves to Terah and his son Abram. As we read the genealogy we note that there is a rapid decline in human longevity after the flood. Noah lives 950 years, but Shem only lives 600 years. His son Arphaxad manages a mere 438 years, followed by a few generations that lived to the mid-400's. By the time of Abram it was down to roughly 120 years.

Assuming the Bible is accurate, why do we only live 70-90 years now? The turning point seems to be the worldwide flood. Could it have been the physical properties of the world that changed lifespan? That does not seem plausible.

Modern genetics may provide the answer. For instance, we understand why it is unwise to have children later in life. That is because mutations in the germ cells build up over time from radiation and other causes. If you look at the age that children began to be born to early humans, we find the normal range of 70 to 180 years. Then we look at Noah, whose children (at least the ones on the ark) were born when he was at least 500 years old. That would be the equivalent of a modern woman waiting until age 40 or 45 to have children. The chances of birth defects increase dramatically at those ages. Even when you start with excellent genetics, mutations enter the reproductive cells and are passed on in increasing numbers as the parents age.

Enter the flood and the ark. On the other side, there are only three breeding pairs of humans left. All of the males were born to elderly parents and presumably have a higher incidence of mutations than their female partners. The population bottleneck of three couples concentrates the defective genes in their offspring and leads to shorter and shorter lifespans until an equilibrium is reached of roughly 120 years by the time of Terah and Abram.

As an aside, God states something in Genesis 6:3 that may explain this particular lifespan at this point in history. 'Then the LORD said, "My Spirit will not contend with humans forever, for they are mortal ; their days will be a hundred and twenty years."' It may just be that the ark took 120 to plan and build, but that coincidence of years does make me wonder if God meant to reduce the human lifespan.

Abram and the Origins of Israel

Terah leaves his home city of Ur of the Chaldees with the intent of going to the territory of Canaan. We are not specifically told why he leaves Ur for Canaan. Instead of completing his journey, he stops at Haran and settles there with his family.

After Terah's death, his son Abram is visited by God, who tells him to leave his extended family and home in Haran and go west to a destination that God will show him. God plans to make a great nation from him that will bless the nations of the world. This has a similar feel to the time God told Noah to build an ark, and then God would make his covenant with Noah. In other words, the promise of a later covenant based on a condition being met first.

This sounds like the offer of a lifetime, so Abram packs up his own family and his nephew Lot and heads west, eventually settling in Canaan, which turns out to have been his father's intended destination. Could it be that Terah was the one God originally intended to form Israel from? Did Terah decide that the journey was too hard and quit? We may never know.

Once they arrive in Canaan, God tells Abram that his descendants will inherit that land, though he will live in it as a resident alien for the rest of his life.

The only "small" snag is that his wife is unable to bear children, making it hard to believe that Abram will have the required descendants. Notice that there is still no covenant yet, just promises so far.

God appears to Abram in a dream, and Abram points out that he has no heir through whom God could fulfil that promise. God tells Abram that he will have a son from his own body. To show that His promise is serious, God asks Abram for a specific kind of sacrifice, requiring animals to be split in half and the two halves placed so that there is a path between them. God appears in the form of a blazing fire, and "walks" the path between the halves.

Bible readers and scholars puzzled over this strange story until archaeologists discovered documents outlining how ancient covenants were made between a conquering king or emperor and the king of a conquered vassal nation. In some cases covenants were ratified by having the vassal walk between halves of slaughtered animals. The warning implied was that failing to abide by the rules of the covenant would result in the severe punishment of being cut in half by the overlord. Clearly God is establishing a covenant with Abram at this point (Genesis 15). In case we did not catch that from the offering it is made clear in verse 18.

The astonishing thing is that *God Himself* walked between the pieces. That makes *God responsible* for the outcome if He does not fulfill the obligations. This is a heavy-duty oath that God binds Himself to on behalf of a normal, not-particularly-righteous, human being. God literally puts His life on the line to show how serious He is about this covenant.

Since Sarai is barren she suggests a solution: a surrogate mother (as a secondary wife) in the form of her servant Hagar. This was allowed under the rules of the nation they left (another law confirmed by archaeology). The not-so-artificial insemination occurs, and a child is born, when Abram is 86 years old. They name him Ishmael. What Sarai and Abram do not realize is that God has other plans for fulfilling the promise to Abram.

A few years later God, accompanied by two people we later learn are angels, visits Abram and Sarai. He informs them that by that time a year later, Sarai will have a son from her own body, and that this son will be the heir of all the promises. They share a meal together and the angels take their leave, heading east to the plain across the Jordan River.

God takes the moment to tell Abram that the angels are heading to investigate reports that there is great evil going on in the cities of the plain, especially in Sodom and Gomorrah. If their investigation proves the allegations are true, these cities will be destroyed. Abram, knowing that his nephew Lot is living among them, asks if God will spare the cities if 50 righteous people can be found among them. God agrees. Abram keeps lowering the number until God agrees not to destroy it if 10 righteous people live there.

The story turns to the angelic investigation of Sodom. They arrive near sundown and prepare to spend the night in the city square. Lot sees them and asks them to spend the night as his guest. As they are eating together the entire population of the city surround his house, demanding that Lot send out his guests so that they can gang rape the angels. He tries to reason with them, but as the crowd moves to break in, the angels intervene and strike the crowd blind.

The angels have seen everything they need to know. This is a violent and evil people who prey on those they perceive as defenseless. They literally drag Lot, his wife and two daughters out of the city and God destroys it by fire from above. Lot's wife, who had been told not to look back, is turned into a pillar of salt, and the three remaining family members find shelter in the surrounding mountains.

God later performs a miracle and allows Sarai, at age 90, to have a baby boy for her 100-year-old husband. God changes the names of the two to Abraham and Sarah. Abraham's name will now reflect the fact that he will be the father of multiple powerful nations, and Sarah will be the mother of many of those nations, and that kings will come from her.

Why does God use a couple who can't even have children to make a nation for Himself? Remember that at the Tower of Babel he divides the nations by language and has them separate from each other across the world. Also remember that he assigns angelic "princes" to lead them with the intent of creating peaceful and just societies. After letting them lead the nations after Babel, we see a clue in Psalm 82 that all is not well in those nations. God "renders judgment among the 'gods,'" stating that they are "defending the unjust" and "showing partiality to the wicked."

Compare this to the description of God in Psalm 89:14. "Righteousness and justice are the foundation of your throne; love and faithfulness go before you." So how will God prove to both humans and "gods" that He will rule fairly and compassionately? By creating a nation that will come under His exclusive rule. He will show the "gods" what righteousness and justice are all about through that people.

But why start with a couple who cannot have children? What He is doing is literally ***creating*** a nation *for Himself* from the most insignificant people you can imagine when it comes to nation-building - a childless couple. He does this to show the rest of the world who He is, the one and only true Creator God. The miracle baby is named Isaac, and for purposes of the covenant, he is to be considered Abraham's "only" son.

Their "only" son Isaac becomes the one through whom God's promise to Abraham will be fulfilled. God makes an unconditional promise that Isaac will be the progenitor of the nation that will inherit Canaan.

Then God does the most unbelievably unconscionable thing you can do to a parent. He tells Abraham that he must travel three days to Mount Moriah and sacrifice his son Isaac there to Himself. Remember that God *promised* that Isaac would be the father of the nation that would inherit the land. Isaac isn't married yet and has no children, legitimate or otherwise, so how is *that* supposed to happen?

What is going on here? What kind of a God is this? What is even stranger is that Abraham prepares the very next day to do exactly that. The reader wonders what kind of parent Abraham is, too. The writer of the book of Hebrews believes that Abraham recognizes that God, as Creator and Life-giver, has something up His metaphorical sleeve. We will see what he says later.

Off they go, father and son. The son has no clue that he is about to be slaughtered until his father literally ties him up, puts him on the altar and brings out the knife. At the last possible second God tells him to stop, and provides a ram as a substitute for the sacrifice. God then tells Abraham that because he was willing to offer his "only" son, the "one he loves," that God will bless him beyond measure without conditions.

The reader wonders what the point of that whole episode is until it becomes clear much later in the story of Jesus Christ. Unfortunately we need to get there in the right order. Let it suffice for the moment to say that God is not asking Abraham to do anything that God Himself is not willing to do. Before we get to that, there is a lot of story to tell about a special nation literally created by God.

After Sarah dies, Abraham sends his most trusted servant to find a wife for his son Isaac among his relatives in Haran. The servant prays, and the prayer is answered with Rebekah, the granddaughter of Nahor, Abraham's brother. After some negotiation with her brother Laban, she accompanies the servant to meet Isaac. They both fall in love at first sight and are soon married.

After Abraham's death and burial beside his wife Sarah, we learn a little bit more about Ishmael's family. He has 12 sons who eventually become nations of their own. They turn out to be much like their father, hard to get along with. They also live in hostile relationships with their relatives.

In the meantime, somehow the men of Abraham's family just can't seem to find women who are able to bear children. Rebekah, like Sarah before her, is barren. How can this be an answered prayer? At this point, you begin to suspect that God has a sense of humor. He is constantly making things happen in ways you do not expect.

After almost 20 years of marriage, Isaac prays on Rebekah's behalf to God, and she becomes pregnant. There is none of this surrogate mother business between them this time. Isaac seems to have learned *that* lesson from his parents. This is one couple dedicated to each other only. Once again God does it His own unique way. They ask for a child, and God gives them a two-for-one deal.

When it seems like there is turmoil going on in her womb, Rebekah asks God what is going on in there, and He actually answers. God tells her that she is carrying twins, and that they will give rise to two very different nations. There will be constant struggle, but the older will end up serving the younger. She believes God but is also not above trying to help things along. This is one thing she has in common with her mother-in-law.

Esau comes out first, with Jacob firmly grasping his heel on the way out, indicating that the younger one will always be struggling to be first in life. The "heel grabber" does end up on top, but his scheming nature makes the journey much harder than it needs to be. He will later meet his match in his uncle Laban, another schemer.

Jacob encounters a hungry Esau one day while he is eating a lentil stew. Esau asks for some stew and Jacob offers to sell it to him in exchange for his birthright. Clearly Esau lives in the moment and does not care about his birthright, so he agrees to the exchange. Score one for the schemer.

Soon afterward, Rebekah overhears her husband telling Esau that he wants to confer his blessing on him once Esau returns from hunting and cooks him supper from the wild meat. At this point Isaac is old and blind, so Rebekah has Jacob bring her two goats, which she prepares just the way Isaac likes. She fastens goat-skins on Jacob's arms to simulate the hairier Esau's arms. She then sends Jacob in with the meal so that Jacob can receive the blessing in place of Esau. She knows that God told her Jacob is supposed to be the one blessed, but this way of going about it is completely dishonest, and Jacob will pay for it for years to come.

The plan succeeds, leaving Esau angry and frustrated with his supplanting brother as there is no more blessing for him. Oddly enough, Isaac seems not to mind that his other son has been deceitful, and refuses to withdraw the blessing he originally intended for Esau from Jacob. He must have realized that he had almost made a mistake. Meanwhile, Esau plots revenge, waiting for the time of his father's death. This is another thing overheard by Rebekah, so she convinces Isaac to send Jacob away to Haran to find a wife. She hopes that Esau will cool off if given enough time. Little does she realize how much time will go by before he returns. Rebekah would never see her son again before she dies.

On the way to Haran, God visits Jacob in a dream and promises to bless and prosper him, to return him safely to his family. Jacob makes a vow that if God does as he promises, Jacob will give him 10% of everything he earns. He carries on with more confidence to Haran, where he meets Rachel, whom he loves at first sight and eventually marries. She is living in the care of her brother Laban the son of Isaac's cousin Bethuel. He agrees to work for Laban as a shepherd for 7 years to gain the hand of Rachel in marriage.

After 7 years the wedding date arrives, and the wily Laban substitutes Rachel's older sister Leah for Rachel as the bride. The veil must have been pretty thick, and the wine must have been flowing pretty freely, because Jacob manages to spend the night with Leah before waking up and realizing he had been duped. Laban's excuse? By their custom he can't have the younger daughter married before the older one.

A distraught Jacob agrees to work another 7 years for Rachel, and is married to her also at the end of the same week that he married Leah. This leads to a lifetime of marital and family strife. Leah feels neglected because Jacob favors Rachel with his affections. She asks God for help, and he provides her with the ability to have four sons, while Rachel remains barren. Rachel gets jealous and offers Bilhah her maid as a surrogate, who has two sons. Leah offers her maid Zilphah, who also has two sons. Leah has two more sons and a daughter, followed by Rachel, who finally has two of her own. Rachel's last child, Benjamin, would be born once the family finally settles in Canaan, in tragic circumstances. The final score in this game of "have the most kids" will be Leah with 6 boys and one girl, and the rest with 2 boys each. Leah "wins" with 7 kids.

Jacob will have a total of 13 children. The 12 boys will end up being the progenitors of the 12 tribes of Israel. Now is the time for Jacob to gain his fortune. He strikes yet another deal with his father-in-law. He will work for Laban for the undesirably marked sheep and goats with streaks or spots. Jacob agrees and Laban secretly removes those from his flock before Jacob can count them, leaving only the ones Laban can claim for himself.

Undaunted, Jacob takes over the flocks and institutes a breeding program that identifies and selectively breeds the sheep and goats for his desired markings and strength. He separates them from Laban's flocks to keep his own healthy and productive. In this way he grows increasingly prosperous, and Laban becomes jealous.

Eventually Jacob and his wives notice that Laban is increasingly irritable and they decide to leave without notifying Laban. A tense confrontation ensues when Laban finds out they have left and he decides to attack. When he arrives he tells Jacob that God had warned him in a dream the previous night not to harm the family or take anything of theirs. They eat a meal together to seal a covenant of non-aggression and part ways peacefully.

Jacob and his family pull up stakes and prepare to meet Jacob's father and brother in Canaan. As they approach, Jacob has another unexpected encounter with the One he will recognize as God. What nobody expects is that it will result in a literal wrestling match with God Himself. What is really unexpected is that Jacob is actually winning when God touches his thigh and Jacob pulls a tendon. Even with a wrenched hip Jacob refuses to let go until he receives a blessing from the stranger. God blesses him and changes his name to Israel, which means, "he struggles with God." This name would truly match the character of the people who would bear that name as a nation.

Jacob prepares to meet his brother Esau by preparing a series of gifts, only to find his brother happy to finally see him again. By this time Rebekah his mother has died. After an incident involving the rape of Dinah, Jacob's daughter, two of his sons embark on a plan of vengeance that wipes out all the men of the city of the offending prince. They loot the city and take the surviving women and children as slaves. This angers the nearby communities of Canaan, so they leave that area.

God tells them to go to Bethel, where God had appeared to Jacob as he was fleeing Esau. God makes a covenant with him there. He tells him to "be fruitful and multiply" and that a nation and a company of nations would arise out of him. Kings would come from his descendants, and that the land God promised Abraham and Isaac would be the possession of his descendants.

Notice that the theme of "be fruitful and multiply" remains consistent in God's covenants throughout Genesis. The idea of being fruitful and multiplying will continue even into what we now call the "new covenant," though in a different form and process.

Shortly afterward Jacob's beloved Rachel gives birth to her final child and dies immediately after Benjamin is born. This child will be the father of Israel's twelfth tribe. Some time after that, Jacob's father Isaac dies and both Esau and Jacob arrange his funeral and mourn together. After this we find out more about Esau's family, and then the story moves on to Jacob's descendants, concentrating on Judah and Joseph in particular. Theirs would be the tribes given the richest blessings of the Abrahamic covenant.

At this point in the account, Judah is mentioned only in terms of how his daughter-in-law Tamar brings his heirs into the world. Judah has three sons from a Canaanite wife, Er, Onan and, considerably later, Shelah. Judah finds a wife, Tamar, for his son Er. Er is so evil that God kills him, leaving Tamar a widow. Judah asks Onan to "help" her produce an heir for his brother Er. He sleeps with her, but uses a primitive form of birth control to prevent her from bearing a child. God considers this to also be evil and kills him, too.

Judah asks her to go back to her father's house and wait until Shelah is old enough to marry her. He is naturally more than a little concerned that he might lose his third and last son, so he does not invite her back when Shelah is old enough. With her biological clock ticking, she notices the snub and decides to solve the heir problem herself.

She disguises herself as a prostitute and waits for him as he is travelling to shear his sheep. A widower himself, he decides not to pass up the opportunity to release some of his tension. She convinces him to part with a couple of personally identifying items as a deposit and returns home. Judah wonders why the prostitute disappears before payment is received. Three months later he hears that Tamar is pregnant and believes he can be free of the commitment to her as a result of her "prostitution." She pulls out the staff and seal he had given her, and he realizes that she was "more righteous" than he had been and accepts her into his household. He does not sleep with her again, but she does bear him twin sons, Perez and Zerah, who replace the evil Er and Onan as heirs, along with their half-brother Shelah.

By far the bulk of the story is about Joseph. Joseph is the unwise kid who learns wisdom when his jealous brothers sell him into slavery. In Egypt he becomes first a model household slave, then a model prisoner when he is unjustly accused of attempted rape by his owner's wife (after rejecting her advances). After some time in prison he accurately interprets the prophetic dreams of two new prisoners, and is eventually rewarded by an audience with Pharaoh, for whom he interprets another prophetic dream about seven years of plenty followed by seven years of famine.

Pharaoh puts Joseph in charge of disaster mitigation, and eventually in charge of the entire nation as Egypt's Prime Minister. His authority was exceeded only by Pharaoh himself, who trusted Joseph completely in all matters of state. When Joseph reveals himself to his family, Pharaoh insists on providing Joseph's family with the best land in Egypt for resettlement to preserve them during the famine.

As Jacob prepares for his own departure from the land of the living, he assembles his sons and pronounces blessings on each of them, along with a prophetic announcement. He reserves special blessings for two of his sons, Judah and Joseph. First, his blessing on Joseph is delivered via Joseph's sons Ephraim and Manasseh, whom he adopts as his own children for purposes of inheritance (bypassing their father, in a sense). This has the effect of giving Joseph a double portion of land inheritance in what will later become the nation of Israel. The blessing includes military might and the most abundant prosperity among all the tribes of Israel.

He then gathers the rest of his sons and pronounces their blessings. The most important one for Christians rests on Judah. Not only will Judah be a militarily powerful and prosperous tribe, but "the scepter will not depart from Judah, nor the ruler's staff from between his feet, until he to whom it belongs shall come and the obedience of the nations shall be his." The kings promised to Abraham and Sarah will be delivered through the tribe of Judah, and so will the ultimate blessing: the King of Kings and Lord of Lords.

Jacob is buried in his father's tomb in Canaan and Joseph reassures his brothers that he will not take vengeance on them for selling him into slavery those years before. He will provide for them, with Pharaoh's blessing, because God wanted Joseph to preserve his family from the famine. After living to see Ephraim's grandchildren and Manasseh's children, Joseph dies at age 110 and is buried in a tomb in Egypt. He had made his brothers swear to have their descendants take his bones with them when they depart Egypt at the appointed time centuries later.

What have we learned about God so far from the book of Genesis?

We learn that God is Creator, obviously. He does it quickly and efficiently, with recognizable design, and establishes an order that works harmoniously and beautifully. While the Bible has much to say about Israel, we learn that God's concern is universal. From the very beginning He works in the whole world as its Creator and Sustainer. Even when humanity begins to go astray God works to continue His plan by activating a contingency wherein humanity will be brought back by the work of individuals working in the world. He works through the family of Adam, sustains the world through Noah's family and eventually chooses a childless couple, Abram and Sarai. From them He will literally *create* a nation from which will come a "seed" that will "bless" all the peoples of the world. His goal is to have a human family who will "bear the image of God" while ruling the created order on God's behalf.

We learn that God can and does work one-on-one with individuals, even though He is Supreme God of the entire created universe. In other words, in spite of His power and greatness, He is a relational, personable God who is interested in relating to individuals as a mentor and friend. This relational aspect of God is awe-inspiring and wonderful, but also extremely frightening.

Because God is actually interested in how we are doing and is also our Creator, He is interested in our thinking and behavior as individuals. The frightening thing is that He has the right to judge both our thinking and our behavior. I doubt that there can be anything more frightening than being judged by the only Being with ultimate power. He can - and did - wipe out an entire planet-full of people on the basis of that judgment, yet he saved one family because of a commitment He made to Eve that one of her descendants would redeem the world from the Serpent's thrall.

God is also frightening due to being willing to put His people to the test of obedience. Adam and Eve had a simple test, but failure had wide-ranging implications for the rest of humanity. Noah had to build an ark, or we would not be here. Abraham had to be willing to sacrifice the son God had promised him. Are we willing to do as He says, no matter what? The choice is not always easy.

Redemption and judgment are both characteristics of the God of Abraham. We need to remember that God has the right as Creator to judge as He sees fit. The God who worked miraculously for Abraham and saved Lot also destroyed Sodom and Gomorrah. We can work with or against Him, but each of those choices has consequences.

The fact that God can judge also says something fundamentally important about human beings. We were created to be able to exercise godly judgment in our creation-based responsibilities. In other words, we are designed to be moral agents in the management of our environment. We are designed to both be good and do good. The fact of God judging implies a moral agency on our part, an ability to choose to do what is good according to God's definition of good or, in biblical language, "righteousness."

This is extremely important, since we must understand what it means to be human if we want to understand what God expects of us. We are made in God's image and therefore have God-like influence on the world around us. We are able to reason, to understand, to create and build, but without "righteousness" what does all of that lead to?

It leads to the violence that preceded the Flood. It leads to the empire-building and domination of people by Nimrod and the building of the Tower of Babel. It leads to the debauchery and dehumanization of the sexual perversion of Sodom, Gomorrah and the other cities of the plain. God intervenes when "unrighteousness" gets completely out of hand. Only being close to God and His teaching can lead us away from the dehumanizing effects of what the Bible calls "sin." Sin is the enemy of all that is truly human in God's eyes.

We also learn that there is a pattern in how God operates. First God elects (chooses individuals or peoples) those who He wants to serve in special capacities. God then saves those individuals or nations. Then those humans respond with worship and faith. Finally, God enters into covenant with them. This will be important to keep in mind as one reads the rest of the Bible.

4

Moses and Israel

The story of how God fulfills the promise to free His people from Egypt is taken up in the book of Exodus. We are told that a pharaoh arises who is unimpressed by Joseph's legacy and that of the rapidly growing family of Israel. Afraid of their power and growing influence he seeks advice about how to prevent them from dominating Egypt. His advisors suggest engaging them as laborers, enslaving them by stealth. Then they can exhaust them with forced labor to slow their reproduction.

Unfortunately this backfires and they multiply even more rapidly, bringing Egypt's leaders to near panic. Pharaoh then orders Hebrew midwives to murder all male children as they are being born. They find excuses to avoid doing so, claiming that Hebrew women give birth too easily and that they can't get there in time to help deliver the boys. God blesses them by allowing Pharaoh to believe the obviously false story. So he has to intervene and order all Egyptians to find all Hebrew baby boys and throw them into the Nile to drown them.

Many Israelite boys died at that time, but God had special plans for one of the baby boys in those dark days.

A woman gave birth to a boy and hatched a plan to try to save him by floating him in a basket on the Nile river. The boy's sister, Miriam, watched from shore as the bundle floated downstream and was found by the daughter of the pharaoh. Seeing that he was a beautiful child, she adopts him and names him Moses. Miriam steps forward and offers to find a wet-nurse for the baby and runs to bring her mother for the job.

Moses has the best of both worlds, raised by a princess and his own birth mother. He learns both Hebrew and Egyptian lore and is further educated in the palace, becoming a prince of Egypt. Naturally, Moses learns to read and write as a member of the most privileged class in the country. This will serve him well as he serves God later in his true vocation.

The idea that some have that Moses was illiterate and could not have written the Torah (five "books of Moses") is complete nonsense. No illiterate rulers could have ruled a kingdom as large and powerful as Egypt at the time. Their scribes would have taken complete advantage of them and ruined them in the process.

Moses is later seen killing a particularly harsh Egyptian slave master who is beating a Hebrew and must flee the country. Like Jacob before him, he meets a beautiful woman at a well and is taken into her father's family. Unlike Laban, Moses' father-in-law Reuel (also known as Jethro) treats him well and puts him in charge of his flocks. For 40 years Moses lives the mostly peaceful life of a shepherd in the territory of Midian, in what we now call Saudi Arabia.

One day Moses is pasturing the sheep near Mount Horeb (also known as Sinai) when he sees a bush on fire, yet it does not seem to be burning up. As he gets closer, a voice greets him from within the fire, identifying the speaker as the God of Abraham, Isaac and Jacob. God gives him the mission of leading the people of Israel from Egypt to freedom in Canaan, the land God had promised to Abraham centuries before. After arguing with God to the point of God's anger, Moses finally agrees. He is met by his brother Aaron, who becomes Moses' spokesman, and they go back to Egypt.

Pharaoh is less than impressed with Moses' "let my people go" speech and makes life ever harder for the already overburdened Israelites. God unleashes 9 devastating plagues on Egypt and its leaders to prove the point that He is in charge and that He means business. In the meantime he prepares His people for the tenth and final plague by instituting a special meal: Passover.

A one-year-old lamb is to be killed and prepared for supper as the 14th of the first month of the year draws to a close. The Israelites are to take some of the blood from the lamb and paint it onto the doorposts beside and above the doors of their homes. They are to eat the lamb with bitter herbs and remain indoors, fully dressed to travel. When they receive the signal, they are to assemble at the city of Sukkoth and leave Egypt together.

They obey, and God strikes Egypt. The tenth plague, the death of all firstborn in Egyptian families and even cattle and sheep, finally convinces Pharaoh to let them go. The people of Israel are protected from the death of their firstborn because the "destroyer" "passes over" the homes with blood on the doorposts and does not enter.

This special meal will become an annual tradition that is still being observed, though in a modified form, by many Jews today. It celebrates the great exodus from Egypt under the mighty arm of their God. God will incorporate this and other special dates into the calendar He gives to Israel when they gather to enter a covenant with Him. Some of these dates will become important in the life and ministry of Jesus Christ. I will go into those details later.

Pharaoh decides to pursue them and his army corners them between mountains and the Red Sea. God miraculously opens a channel of dry land through the sea, allowing Israel to cross. When Pharaoh realizes this is happening he unwisely sends his chariots and army in pursuit down the channel. At dawn, the last Israelite has crossed and God closes the sea over the advancing army, drowning them all. It has taken three days from Passover night to dawn on the third day for Israel to be completely free of the threat of Egypt.

This three-day journey from the Passover sacrifice to the birth of the nation of Israel from slavery through the "birth canal" of the Red Sea will become the type of Jesus' death and resurrection.

God then has Moses bring them to the base of Mount Sinai, where He enters into a covenant with them after uttering the famous Ten Commandments in His own awesome and frightening voice.

I had mentioned earlier that I would get back to describing the location of Mount Sinai. At this point in the story, I want to point out a bit of geographical illiteracy that has made it impossible to find evidence of the Israelite encampment at Mount Sinai, which is traditionally located at the southern tip of the Sinai Peninsula in Egypt. The problem is that the Sinai Peninsula was never part of the territory of Midian, which was actually located within the territory now called Saudi Arabia.

Do you see the problem? How are you going to find a mountain in Asia when you are looking in Africa? In other words, people are looking on the wrong side of the Red Sea to find Mount Sinai, so of course they will not find evidence of Israel there. One research team has decided to search in Saudi Arabia, and they seem to have finally found evidence in the form of 12 pillar stones at the base of a mountain that appears to have been burned on top. Do a Google search for "Mt. Sinai in Arabia" and you will see what I mean.

Remember? God had met Moses on that very mountain in a burning bush while he was tending sheep for his father-in-law *in Midian*. I was shocked that somebody had to point that out to me after I had read the story many times. I was like the man who is looking for a lost item near a lamppost when a stranger asks if he can help. When the stranger asks where it was lost it he says, "In those bushes over there." "So, why are you looking here?" "Because the light is better," he replies. Everybody says it must be on the Sinai Peninsula, so we automatically look there.

Even the Apostle Paul notes that the location of Mount Sinai was "in Arabia" (Galatians 4:25). Who am I to argue with Paul, that great Jewish leader of the early Gentile Christian Church?

Now that we find ourselves at the base of the real Mount Sinai in Arabia, let us resume the story of Moses and the fledgling nation of Israel.

The famous Ten Commandments uttered by God formed what most consider the backbone of the Old Covenant. That is sort of true, but not for the reasons most think. The original covenant with Israel was spoken by God over what we now call chapters 20 to 23 of the book of Exodus. The people of Israel only heard the Ten Commandments portion of it because they became frightened and left the area. They asked Moses to keep listening on their behalf and convey the rest himself. What was written up and agreed to was the entire package in chapter 24.

Moses goes up the mountain afterward and God carves out two stone tablets, engraving them with the covenant. These would later be replaced because Moses breaks the tablets as he descends the mountain when he discovers that his people are already disobedient to the covenant. It only took 40 days for them to build an idol, a golden calf, and start worshiping before it.

Moses intercedes on the people's behalf (after roundly chastising them). God relents on destroying them and starting over again with Moses. Moses then carves out two tablets like the first and God engraves the covenant on them again. They end up stored in a special box called the "ark of the covenant."

As an aside, it is generally believed that God wrote in very large letters (120 point type?), with 5 commandments on each tablet. What is most likely is that God inscribed the entire covenant on each tablet. This is based on the idea that covenant copies were generally kept in two locations. In normal treaties of that time one copy belonged to the sovereign king while the other is for reference by the vassal king.

Meredith Kline, in his book *Treaty of the Great King* argues emphatically on p. 19 that each of the two tablets had a complete copy of the covenant engraved on it. God was likely making the point that He would dwell among His people, so both copies are kept side-by-side in one place, within God's earthly dwelling-place, the tabernacle. This is why the box it is kept in is referred to as the "ark of the covenant" rather than the "ark of the ten commandments."

The nation was promised that it would eventually have a king. Could it be that God was preparing a copy in advance for Israel's king, who would be a vassal king under the King of Kings, God Almighty? God is certainly well known for His ability to plan ahead.

I have already provided an overview of the rest of the books of Moses (the Law) to describe their travels and refusal to enter the Promised Land after the report of the spies. After wandering in the wilderness for 40 years, Israel was once again at the border of the Promised land. Moses dies and is mourned for 30 days, and Joshua prepares to take them across into the land God promised Abraham, Isaac and Jacob/Israel.

Joshua and the Promised Land

The story continues as Joshua leads Israel across the Jordan river, miraculously stopping the flow so they could cross on dry land. This is followed by the famous, archaeologically confirmed, falling outward of the walls of Jericho. Other battles ensue until Israel occupies the heart of Canaan and only a few holdout cities remain, including Jerusalem.

For the most part, the giants that the previous generation feared so much are almost wiped out, with the few remaining ones fleeing to Philistine cities such as Gath, the home of the famous later giant Goliath. Joshua dies with the nation in Israel's possession and at peace until even the elders who served under him pass on.

The Judges

The period that follows is chaotic, as Israel begins to forget who their true God is. They start following other gods and fall prey to neighboring countries, who first raid them and later start taking over some of their territory. At times they repent and turn back to God or at least cry out to Him. He sends saviors referred to as "judges" (hence the title of the book of Judges).

Time and again they fall into a pattern of straying from God, regretting it and being saved by odd individuals with strange characteristics. Left-handed

Ehud kills a Gentile overlord. Jephtha the illegitimate son and outcast is begged to command the army and repels the Ammonite occupiers of Gilead. Gideon the timid becomes a mighty military commander. Samson the strong man with breathtaking anger issues falls at the hand of Canaanite beauty Delilah, but is granted a final feat of strength that wipes out the elite of the Philistines in one performance that literally brings down the house. Eventually the nation would rally under one final judge who combines priestly, prophetic, teaching and judicial duties: Samuel. Samuel's role would be a turning point in Israel's story. He is the priestly prophet who establishes Israel as a kingdom and anoints its first two kings.

The story of Samuel's birth annoys biblical critics because it is yet another "miracle baby" story. Like Sarah, Rebekah and Rachel before her, Hanna is unable to bear children. Her husband loves her, but has married a second wife, who constantly provokes her about her childlessness. After years of this she is caught praying silently at the tabernacle by Eli the priest, who assumes she is drunk. As he tries to drive her away, she explains that she has been praying. The priest prays a blessing that she receives what she asks for and they both go their own ways.

The family finishes and returns home, and you can guess what happens nine months later. It was tradition for a woman to wean a child over the course of three years, so she stays home with the baby until that time is over. The next time she appears at the tabernacle she surprises Eli with a "gift to the Lord," her son Samuel. She prays an inspired "thank you Lord" prayer that is recorded in full. Eli later prays that Hanna have other children and she goes on to be blessed with three sons and two daughters.

In the meantime Eli adopts the boy Samuel and trains him to be a priest. What is interesting about this is that Samuel seems to come from the wrong blood-line to be a priest. We are told that his father was from the tribe of Ephraim. We are not told that his mother was from Levi or from Aaron's family. God seems to be fine with this "adoption" into the priesthood, which suggests that grace triumphs over law even in the Old Testament. This will be important later when we discuss King David's relationship with the priesthood.

As Samuel grows up he begins to hear God speaking to him, much to the surprise and both joy and dread of Eli. Samuel reluctantly tells Eli that he and his sons are rejected as priests by God and will be replaced by more suitable priests after God wipes them out for their dereliction of duty. A lack of judgment on the part of Eli's sons leads to their death, the capture of the ark of the covenant by the Philistines and the death of Eli when he falls and breaks his neck after hearing the news.

There follows a hilarious interlude during which the Philistines deal with a very problematic ark of the covenant, which seems to bring nothing but embarrassing confrontations with their own idols and painful sores and cancers to the population of whatever city it resides in. They eventually realize that they have no choice but to send it back. The mighty Philistines prove helpless to defeat a box!

Samuel begins to knit a fractured Israel back together as he turns the people back to the LORD. As they come back to God they begin to drive out the surrounding oppressors under Samuel's direction. God keeps Israel's enemies at bay during the rest of Samuel's tenure. For the rest of his career Samuel sets up "schools of the prophets." He also becomes Israel's primary circuit court judge. That is quite the career: priest, judge, prophet and educator.

The Kingdom of Israel

As Samuel's ministry matures, it becomes clear that his sons are nowhere near as close to God as Samuel is, and the people start to notice. They increasingly demand to have a king, like all the nations around. This pleases neither Samuel nor God, who tells Samuel to warn the people about the negative things they can expect. Samuel warns them that taxes, bloated bureaucracy and conscription will increase and get to the point of oppressiveness, and that they will regret that decision.

They still insist on having a king, so God allows it. God chooses a handsome, tall and soldierly man named Saul to be their king. Saul encounters Samuel while looking for a lost donkey. Samuel invites him for supper and tells him not to worry because the donkey has been found. He then informs a disbelieving Saul that he is the king of Israel. As a sign that this is true, he would encounter a group of prophets with their musical instruments by a specific tree on his way back, and he would prophesy with them. It all happens just as Samuel predicts, shaking Saul to the core.

The Bible usually does not add unnecessary detail to its stories, so I was struck by the fact that the prophets were armed with musical instruments. It turns out that music and prophecy have a history of working together. Most modern translations render most prophetic utterances in the Bible in versified form. Many of the prophets used poetry and music to convey their messages from God, and you will find many passages in versified form in the Bible outside of the Psalms, which are clearly intended to be sung. I will say more about that in connection with King David.

Saul is presented to the people at a special service, though he is shy and has to be dragged out of hiding first. The people rejoice, thinking that Saul looks like the kind of king that the other nations have. They think he can protect them from all enemies.

Saul starts well, and wins the first battles against other nations. Unfortunately, he begins to think that he knows better than God and Samuel. He is ordered to wipe out the tribe of Amalek, who had attacked Israel without provocation as Israel attempted to enter the Promised land a few generations before. When Saul spares king Agag and the best of the loot, against God's specific orders, God decides that Saul does not deserve to have a dynasty. Saul's degeneration continues until he takes it upon himself to offer a sacrifice without a Samuel's priestly presence, on the pretext that Samuel was late.

God is not pleased with Saul's arrogance and tells Samuel to find a replacement who can be trained from youth. God chooses David, seventh son of Jesse, and has Samuel secretly anoint him as the next king. David is not what the people would have chosen. He was the runt of the family, a mere shepherd who was treated with disdain by his brothers, some of whom were strong and capable soldiers. David had not even been invited to the supper during which he was anointed until Samuel insisted on seeing him.

On a visit to bring supplies to his brothers on the front lines of a conflict with the Philistines, he discovers the army cowering in fear before the giant, Goliath of Gath. David accepts Goliath's challenge to a one-on-one fight in the name of the LORD. Unfortunately for Goliath, he brought a sword to a sling fight. David hits him between the eyes, knocking him out, then uses Goliath's own sword to cut his head off. This both motivates Israel and demoralizes the Philistines, who are roundly defeated by Israel as they flee.

After a number of other circumstances, David is inducted into the army and becomes a formidable military commander in his own right, outshining even Saul in skill and popularity. Saul becomes jealous and attempts several times to kill him. Saul eventually spends more time hunting down David and his loyal troops than defending the country from enemies because he fears David will replace him as king.

After a disastrous attempt to consult a medium (forbidden in God's law), Saul dies on the battlefield and David is declared king of Judah, Benjamin and Levi. These tribes eventually would be named the Kingdom of Judah. These tribes would remain loyal to the line of David for centuries. After a civil war with Saul's family and their loyalists, David is named king of the remaining tribes. David's troops would finally conquer the city of Jerusalem, which would become the capital of the nation of Israel during his reign and that of his son Solomon.

David, the Priestly King?

David would oversee the establishment of God's tabernacle to its permanent home in Jerusalem and draw up plans to build a permanent building to house God's earthly throne. In a play on words, God responds by telling David that He planned to build David a permanent "house" too - a perpetual dynasty that would be enthroned in Jerusalem.

There are some interesting things to note about David. First of all, like Moses, David spends a formative time in his life as a shepherd. He must eventually learn statecraft under King Saul. Moses, on the other hand, learned statecraft first under Pharaoh and then became humble as a shepherd.

Another interesting feature about David is his musical ability. He played a guitar-like instrument and composed songs both among the sheep and within the royal palace. He is apparently credited with writing a majority of the Psalms, which is more-or-less Israel's hymnal. In other words, David ends up writing a lot of the worship music of his time. For a king, that is quite an unusual accomplishment. How is it that a king gets to influence the worship of God's nation?

It gets even stranger. Remember how Saul is disqualified from kingship for impersonating a priest? In 2 Samuel 6 we find David dressed as a priest, dancing as the ark of the covenant is being brought into Jerusalem and set in place in a tabernacle on Mount Zion. David then actually sacrifices offerings before God and then blesses the people - two other priestly duties! It is following this that God offers David a perpetual dynasty. What is going on here?

It gets even stranger. Once David arranges to have the Levites bring the ark of the covenant into a tent that *David set up for it,* he orders the Levites to set up musical worship teams to minister before the tabernacle (1 Chronicles 15:16 and 16:4). This is something that not even Moses had set up for worship. He even chooses the music for the first service (1 Chronicles 16:7-36). He then sets up a priestly rotation to serve at the tabernacle over the year (1 Chronicles 24:3). All of this seems to please the LORD.

Not even David's descendants were privileged to serve in priestly ways. We never see any of David's descendants wearing the priestly ephod. King Uzziah, much later, tried to enter the Holy of Holies to burn incense and was rewarded by God with leprosy, which made it forbidden for him to ever enter the Temple grounds to worship again. Why was David so special?

Earlier in the Bible we read of encounters with priests of God who were not born of Israel. One of them was Moses' father-in-law Reuel, also known as Jethro. Long before Moses, Abraham also had an encounter with a priest,

Melchizedek, who was also the king of Salem. Once Abraham's small army had defeated the armies that had taken Lot's family and the cities that included Sodom, Abraham was met on the way by Melchizedek, who blessed Abraham. Abraham gave Melchizedek 10% of the spoils of battle as an offering to God.

In this enigmatic figure Melchizedek we find a king who is also a priest of the true God. The city of which he is king is named Salem, which is an early name for Jerusalem. You can probably see where this is going. David, as king of Salem/Jerusalem is a kind of Melchizedek priest/king. God is granting him both a priesthood and a kingdom. The priesthood of Melchizedek is a higher-order priesthood than that of Aaron's family.

While Samuel was adopted into the priesthood, David seems to have had it thrust upon him by God, occasioning Psalm 110, which speaks of a king to whom the LORD swears, "You are a priest forever, in the order of Melchizedek." The writer of the book of Hebrews picks up this quote and applies it to Jesus Christ (Hebrews 7:11-22). David appears to have functioned in a similar ministry as a foreshadow or preview of the Saviour who was to come hundreds of years later.

David and Uriah: The "thing" that displeased God.

Just when you think Israel is on its way to lasting peace and prosperity under David, things start going wrong. At a time when David should be leading the troops in battle, he is lounging around the castle and sees a beautiful (married) woman bathing on the terrace below him. He sends for her, has his way with her, and later discovers she is pregnant. Panic sets in and he attempts to cover up his crime. This fails, so he orders his trusted, but amoral general to make sure her husband, Uriah the Hittite dies in battle. In desperation he marries Bathsheba the widow to cover up the deeds.

Some people read the story and think that Bathsheba deliberately seduced David. In Hebrew literature only the most important details are revealed, and many clues abound to show that David is at fault. For one thing, we don't even learn the name of the woman until David proposes marriage, after she has mourned her husband's death. She probably is not even aware that David did him in. The story prior to that is actually about David and Uriah. We find Uriah loyal to David and his own troops to a fault. He resents being asked to come to the capital while his troops are in the field. David tries unsuccessfully to get him to sleep with his wife while he is in the city, but he refuses due to his loyalty. David is the one who should be loyal to his troops, but he instead sends Uriah back with the letter that seals his doom.

The most ominous words pointed at someone in the Bible are, "The thing displeased the LORD." When God says this you know that David is in deep trouble. David has added murder to his sexual assault and adultery. David and Bathsheba's first child pays the price by dying. David would face continual challenges from within his own family and from other nations for the rest of his life. One of David's own sons would try to kill him to gain his throne. Some of his sons even murder each other in their desire for power or vengeance.

At no point is the literary finger of blame pointed at Bathsheba. In fact, Nathan the prophet catches David's conscience with the story of a man with a large flock who, in order to feed a guest, steals the only sheep of a poor neighbor. David, outraged, says that the man deserves death. Nathan responds, "You are that man." David gets the point. He has stolen the wife of another man for his own use, even though he already had multiple wives of his own.

Not only is she not blamed, but her next son Solomon turns out to be the only son of David worthy of the throne. One has to suspect that God is blessing her in the midst of the tragedy of her previous loss at the hands of her current husband. God makes sure that Solomon becomes the next king of the united Israel. Under the peaceful reign of Solomon Israel would reach its peak in power and prestige, and also sow the seeds of its decline.

5

Israel's Decline and Fall

Solomon starts his reign extremely well, to the point that even God is pleased and offers him anything he wants. Solomon's answer pleases Him even more. What Solomon wants is the wisdom to rule the people of Israel in such a way that they prosper and are blessed.

God is so pleased that He even adds fame and prosperity to Solomon in addition to the wisdom.

Solomon's wisdom and prosperity becomes renowned throughout the ancient world. Dignitaries from faraway lands come to Solomon's court and palace to experience the wisdom and wealth of this famous personage. The Queen of Sheba (modern Ethiopia) is cited as an example of one who was very impressed with Solomon and Israel.

Unfortunately, many diplomatic agreements in those days were ratified by royal intermarriages among nations. Partly as a result of Solomon's canny diplomacy he found himself married to seven hundred (!) wives of royal birth, not counting the 300 concubines ("secondary" wives). One suspects that he should have asked for wisdom in choosing who to marry, too.

Despite the warning in the law of Moses not to marry foreigners lest they turn him to other gods, Solomon ends up worshiping the gods of his foreign wives, angering God. The last straw occurs when Solomon builds altars to Chemosh and Molech, the abominable gods that require child sacrifice. God tells Solomon that the kingdom will be torn out from under him. This turns out to be the beginning of the end of a united Israel, though God decrees that the formal division will occur under the reign of his son Rehoboam.

God stirs up external and internal enemies of Solomon, including one of Solomon's officials, Jereboam, who would later become king over ten of the twelve tribes of Israel during the reign of Rehoboam, Solomon's son.

Rehoboam turns out to be the opposite of his father in terms of diplomacy, and tries to treat the people of Israel in a manner similar to Pharaoh by increasing their workload. Jereboam leads a revolt that takes ten tribes away from Rehoboam's rule, Leaving Rehoboam with Judah, Benjamin, and many of the Levites. Israel is thus divided into two portions, the "House of Judah" and the "House of Israel." The first time the word "Jew" is used in the Bible is in 2 Kings 16:6 in the King James and American Standard versions, where Judah is being attacked by Israel and its ally Aram.

Unfortunately Jereboam sees a problem. Israel's only place of worship resides in Jerusalem, outside of his territory. He does not want people to go back to the heartland of their God to worship, for fear that they will go back to Rehoboam. He sets up an alternative in his own territory. He changes the festival of Tabernacles to the next month and sets up golden calves in the north and south of his kingdom, claiming that these are the gods who brought them out of Egypt.

This sets up a chain of disastrous degeneration in the northern kingdom that leads eventually to its destruction and the scattering of its people, as God predicted. Assyria wipes the House of Israel off the map and carries its people into captivity, replacing them in the land with peoples of other nations. These people become known in the New Testament as the hated rivals of the Jews, the Samaritans.

The southern House of Judah fares somewhat better for a while longer, with alternating righteous and unrighteous kings. In a way, this resembles the time of the Judges, with Judah's decay and regeneration depending on whether their king follows God. Eventually Judah falls apart, and in 586 B.C., it too falls to King Nebuchadnezzar's Chaldean Empire, popularly known as the

Babylonian Empire. Its people are also dispersed within Babylon's territory, which has taken over the then-known "civilized" world.

This is the world that the prophets Jeremiah, Ezekiel and Daniel lived and ministered within. Jeremiah has the unpleasant task of warning unfaithful kings and their nation that God is going to hand them over to a foreign power if they do not repent. Ezekiel the priest and Daniel the prince find themselves taken captive and must function under Babylonian domination, waiting for the time Judah can return to their land.

6

The Return of Judah (Sort of)

Nebuchadnezzar's son and grandson turn out to be inept rulers. The Persians and Medes successfully rebel, allowing these related peoples to take over and create the Medo-Persian Empire, usually called the Persian Empire. Under Cyrus the Persian and Darius the Mede, the Jews are allowed to return to their land and reestablish worship in Jerusalem, eventually building the Second Temple. Daniel lived long enough to serve under both Babylon and Persia, even into the reign of Darius. He must have been exceedingly wise and useful to prosper under such dramatic changes in administration.

The books of Ezra and Nehemiah were written during the Persian rule. Ezra writes of the resettlement of Judah and the struggle to rebuild God's temple and reestablish worship. Ezra the Scribe arrives to a Jerusalem that is straying from God by marrying into the surrounding pagan and semi-pagan peoples. A prophet named Malachi preaches repentance from this and other practices, assisting Ezra in bringing a "national" repentance. The guilty parties send away their pagan wives and agree to a covenant of renewal of obedience to God's law. The closing words of Malachi's prophecy are a prophecy that an "Elijah" would come to announce the coming of the "dreadful day of the LORD." This will come up again in connection with Jesus Christ.

Nehemiah arrives a few years later with a mission to strengthen Jerusalem by rebuilding the wall and fortifications around it. He first scouts out the problems, makes up a plan and announces it to the inhabitants. He rallies and organizes the citizenry and overcomes the opposition from within and from surrounding nations to finish the task.At one point he even organizes the builders in teams with armed men to dissuade potential attackers.

Another crisis comes up when Nehemiah discovers that some of the Jews are oppressing other Jews by forcing them into slavery to buy food during a famine. They were doing so by charging interest, which is forbidden under the law of Moses. Nehemiah first lends money to get some of them out of slavery Nehemiah then confronts the leaders who were doing this in the presence of the priests, and they repent, giving back the interest and the fields they had taken and freeing the remaining slaves.

Once again it is discovered that Jews had married into the pagan nations around them. Nehemiah also leads the people to repent and divorce their pagan wives, including some among the priests! They seal the deal with a binding covenant signed by all the leaders.

During the turbulent time of Ezra and Nehemiah three final prophets arrive on the scene to encourage the rebuilding of the temple and of the city, and to encourage faithfulness to God. I have already mentioned Malachi. The two others were Zechariah and Haggai. Haggai preached mainly to encourage the rebuilding of the temple to a people that had let the project lapse in favour of their own homes and work.

Zechariah also preached about rebuilding the temple but was given several visions about the future of Jerusalem, including some prophecies about the entrance into Jerusalem of a King who would rule the world (Zechariah 9:9). This King would arrive on a donkey ((Zechariah 9:9, Matthew 21:5). Another prophecy is about the pittance that would be paid as the value for God - 30 pieces of silver (Zechariah 11:12-13; Matthew 26: 14-15 and 27:1-10). In this case Zechariah may have been quoting a verbal prophecy of Jeremiah rather than a written one. In any case, Jesus is sold out for 30 pieces of silver and the cash is used to buy the potter's field that Judas hangs himself in.

The book of Esther highlights the troubles that God predicted in Deuteronomy 28. The Jewish and Israelite peoples would never be free of problems and trials in the lands in which they were scattered. Esther, a Jewish woman, becomes the queen of Persia due to achieving first place in a beauty contest she was forced to participate in by the authorities. Shortly afterward a man named Haman the Agagite (from the Edomite tribe of Amalek, Israel's longtime enemy) becomes chief advisor to King Xerxes. He convinces the king to sign an edict enforcing extermination of the Jewish people within Persia.

Esther's uncle Mordecai finds out about the plot and convinces Esther to reveal her true nationality. She risks her life to gain an audience with the king, then risks it again by revealing her identity. The king is infuriated with Haman, but cannot undo the extermination decree. Mordecai suggests, through Esther, that the Jews be warned and allowed to defend themselves, and the king grants Mordecai his signet ring to create the decree in the king's name. The Jews wipe out their intended exterminators and gain power and prestige in the eyes of the nation - for a time.

Persia falls to the Graeco-Macedonian Empire of Alexander the Great, whose kingdom falls into the hands of four of his generals at Alexander's death in 323 B.C. They split the kingdom four ways, and struggles ensue among the four until two of them dominate, the Ptolomaic and Seleucid kingdoms. Judah finds itself in the control of one, then the other, until the Seleucid king Antiochus Epiphanes tries to destroy their religion. The final straw is the attempt to set up an idol of Jupiter Olympus (Zeus) in God's Temple. This sets off a guerrilla movement among the Jews that eventually drives out the Greek rulers for a brief time, until Rome crushes Judea and takes over.

7

Jesus and Judea

Judea was a Roman vassal kingdom when Jesus was born. The Jewish people were struggling under an increasingly heavy tax burden and the oppressive force of the Roman military occupation. They were looking for a David-like military commander and king who would drive out the Romans. Several pretenders had already tried and failed, bringing the Roman yoke more oppressively on the remnant of Israel.

It was into this world that Jesus the son of Joseph and Mary was born. An Idumean nobleman named Herod "the Great" had been appointed King of Judea by the Roman overlords. He was from the people of Jacob's brother Esau rather than a Jew. The man was both arrogant and paranoid, a dangerous combination in a king. He was so paranoid that he arranged to have much of his own family killed because he feared being deposed by one of them.

One fine day an elderly priest named Zechariah is at work in the temple in Jerusalem. He was married to a descendant of Aaron named Elizabeth. Unfortunately, her priestly pedigree did not make her immune to barrenness, so they had no children. (Here we go again!) They were both very faithful to God and His law. Zechariah was serving in the temple, lighting the incense burner, when he was startled by an unexpected visitor.

This visitor, an angel of the LORD, brings him the welcome news that they would have a son. This son, whom they were to name John, would become a mighty prophet. John would work "in the spirit and power of Elijah, to turn the hearts of parents to their children" (Luke 1:5-17). The angel identifies himself as Gabriel, who had previously met Daniel to help him understand some of his visions.

Because Zechariah does not immediately believe, Gabriel takes away his voice. Zechariah returns home after his appointed service and soon his wife becomes pregnant in her old age. Zechariah remains voiceless until the birth of the child, when he is asked what the child's name would be. He writes, "His name is John." Immediately his ability to speak returns, and he breaks into a prophetic song about the boy and of praise to God.

In the meantime, a young virgin named Mary, a descendant of King David, was engaged to be married. She was a faithful believer in the LORD. Her parents had arranged for her to be married to a man named Joseph, another descendant of David, though the wedding was still in the future. One evening she is visited by the same angel who had visited Daniel centuries before. He announces that she would be the mother of God's own Son, by being impregnated by means of the Holy Spirit. She humbly accepts the responsibility of bearing and rearing God's own Son and it happens as predicted. Jesus becomes the ultimate miracle baby!

Mary finds out that her elderly cousin Elizabeth is also pregnant, and goes to stay with her until Elizabeth gives birth six months later. Mary then returns home, clearly showing her own pregnancy. How is Joseph going to react?

As the wedding day approaches, Joseph can't help but notice the "baby bump" that Mary is sporting. Thinking that she has cheated on him, he decides to quietly annul the marriage. (Considering that the alternative is stoning her to death, this seems to be a kinder solution.) Fortunately God sends an angel to apprise him of the change of plans and he rolls with it. They get married, but delay having sex until the child is born so that the virgin birth can be quietly noted by the midwives and family.

As Mary approaches the time to give birth, Augustus Caesar proclaims that all Jews must return to their family birthplace to be counted in a census. Jesus is born in the sleepy town of Bethlehem, the city of David. Because of the census, the inns are filled to capacity. Fortunately the small business owner of one of them accommodates the couple, and Jesus is perhaps literally born in a barn.

Angels appear to a group of shepherds in a nearby field and announce the birth of the Messiah in town. They disturb the entire town while looking for the newborn king, and finally find him sleeping in a feeding trough, or "manger."

The couple later moves to a house, where they are met by a very special group of high-ranking foreigners called "magi." These men had come from the east, from Parthia, a nation that emerged from the former Persian empire. They had a formidable military force, and had come to a stalemate with the Roman Empire. Neither side could convincingly overpower the other side, and they eventually used the Euphrates River as their common boundary.

These men were the wise men or sages of the Parthian empire, the ones who determined who should be the next king of that empire. They were philosophers, astronomers, astrologers - the scientists of their time. They were also the advisors to the kings. These were Very Important People. This was definitely not three guys on camels who sneak into the country and somehow get to see King Herod. This was a delegation of high-powered dignitaries from a foreign and somewhat hostile superpower. When they arrived, they were accompanied by a royal retinue including servants, a caravan bearing gifts, and a large armed escort of professional soldiers. These are the kind of visitors that get a king's attention - and an audience.

The other thing that we need to know is that King Herod achieved his high rank under the Romans by being instrumental in helping the Romans repel a Parthian invasion some years before. These people represented an enemy he had once faced in battle. Needless to say, their presence made him somewhat nervous. Their request to meet the king who would replace him certainly fed his paranoia.

Let's pause for a moment and consider why this strange delegation of very important foreigners is interested in a newborn "king of the Jews." As noted, these were magi, the elite philosopher/astronomer/scientists of the time, who came from the territory of the old Persian Empire. These were the descendants and recruits of the same people that advised the previous Babylonian and Persian kings, who were now advising the Parthian kings.

They once had a very special leader in the days of Nebuchadnezzar of Babylon and Cyrus and Darius of Persia - none other than Daniel the Prophet/Magus. Nebuchadnezzar had appointed him both Governor of Babylon Province and Chief of the Magi. Unlike many others, Daniel continued serving in both roles in the Persian Empire. Daniel would have taught them what to watch for in the future of Judah, based on revelations of God.

The prophet/wise man Daniel had been informed by an angel of God that there would be "seventy sevens" of years decreed for Jerusalem from the year a decree went out to rebuild the city. It was to be in the 483rd year that the Messiah would be introduced to the Jewish people in Jerusalem. This messiah would be killed by a people who would eventually give rise to a king who would challenge even God at the end of the world as we know it. (Not the destruction of the globe, just the establishment of the Kingdom of God.)

They would have been watching for a "star rising out of Jacob" and "a scepter rising out of Israel" (Numbers24:17). In other words, *they already had a general time frame and a nation to watch* for a King who would rule the world. They had come to *worship* this king.

Herod asks his Jewish priests if they knew where this king would be born, and they respond instantly, "Bethlehem." He provides the visitors with the information and asks that they return once they see this king and tell Herod where to find the child. Naturally he does not actually want to worship this young Jewish king, but rather to kill him.

Herod's scribes knew where Jesus would be born because of an ancient Israelite prophecy in Micah 5:2. Yet another prophet taught where he would be brought up: Nazareth (Matthew 2:23). Another prophecy indicated where the bulk of his ministry of bringing light into darkness would occur: Galilee of the Gentiles (Isaiah 9:1).

The Magi bring expensive gifts worthy of a king and priest to the boy's parents and go their way. God warns them not to go back to Herod, so they go back home. God also warns Joseph to pack up his family and head to Egypt because Herod will not be happy. Herod kills all of the children two years old and under in Bethlehem, hoping to kill the upstart baby king before he can overthrow Herod. Herod is acting almost exactly like the Egyptian Pharaoh who killed baby Israelite boys to prevent them from taking over Egypt.

Once word reaches Joseph via angelic messenger service that Herod is dead, they return to Judea, only to find one of Herod's surviving sons as ruler in place in Jerusalem. Joseph decides to head north and they settle in Nazareth near the Sea of Galilee.

Jesus grows up among the Jews and Gentiles of Roman-occupied Galilee, increasing in wisdom and people skills. He learns his father's trade of carpentry, which also involved some stone masonry. He travels yearly with the family for Passover to Jerusalem, and spends a few days among the priests at the Temple answering tough biblical questions and impressing the priests with his knowledge and wisdom at the age of 12.

At age 30 he goes to the prophet John the Baptist (yet another miracle baby born to an elderly, otherwise childless, cousin of Mary). John points him out as Israel's Messiah. He calls Jesus the "Lamb of God who takes away the sin of the world." If you have managed to read the entire Bible to this point it is hard to miss the obvious Passover lamb overtones of this description. Suffice it to say that this is not usually good news for the lamb that is the "chosen one" at Passover time.

After His introduction as Israel's Messiah by John the Baptist Jesus is led into the Judean wilderness by the Holy Spirit (Matthew 4 and Luke 4). He is tempted by Satan and succeeds in doing what Adam did not do: obey God rather than the "serpent." At the end of the discussion, Jesus tells Satan to leave and the serpent obeys. This establishes for the reader that Jesus, unlike Adam, has dominion over the creatures, even the Devil. The writer of the Hebrews points to the contrast between Jesus and all other human beings beginning with a quote from Psalm 8.

> *What is man that you are mindful of him?*
> *Or a son of man that you care for him"*
> *You made him a little lower than the angels;*
> *Yet you crowned him with glory and honor*
> *And put everything under his feet. (verses 4-6)*

He then goes on to describe how we do not see all things in subjection to mankind, yet we see Jesus Christ in charge now, especially now that He is resurrected from the dead (Hebrews 2:6-9). Of course, other clues that Jesus has dominion on behalf of mankind come from walking on water and calming the stormy wind and waves. The disciples marvel, thinking, "Who is this? He commands even the wind and the water, and they obey." (Luke 8:25 NIV)

Jesus' teaching frustrated both conservative and liberal Jews of his time. The conservative Pharisees did not like his attacks on their addition of extra rules as a "hedge" to "protect" people from accidentally violating God's law. They also resented His "self-proclaimed" authority to interpret God's law. These are the ones that he tells to stop judging others, lest they be judged by the same measure by which they themselves judge others.

The liberal Sadducees, the priestly class, also resented his interpretations of the law. They resented the fact that he knew the law and applied its principles better than they did. They also resented His breaking up of the marketplace set up in the Temple to exchange Roman coinage for "temple coinage" at a considerable profit for the priests.

The Herodians, loyal to the Herod Antipas in Galilee, son of Herod the Great, thought Jesus was going to attempt to overthrow the Roman government. That would put them out of business as Roman sycophants. They, like the other two groups, wanted Jesus out of the way.

These three groups, who normally were at odds with each other, found common cause in trying to undermine Jesus' influence with the masses. They all agreed that Jesus posed a threat to their common pro-Roman stance by virtue of his apparent messianic teaching and miracle-working. The Pharisees and Sadducees tried to trick Jesus with questions about the law of Moses. After Jesus repeatedly handed their rhetorical backsides to them, they finally gave up and wanted to get rid of him.

Jesus' message of peace and human brotherhood did not please the anti-Roman fanatics either. Jesus warns the people of Judea that if they follow the example of certain Galileans and people of Siloam against the Romans that they need to repent before they also are killed in the same manner. What many readers of the New Testament do not notice is that warning the people against opposition to the Roman occupation is also at the heart of his messages about "going the extra mile" and "turning the other cheek."

God had put the "evil" Romans in charge because of Israel's past and present (in His day) rebellion against God. If they had understood the book of Daniel they would have understood that the era of Gentile rule over Israel would extend until God Himself intervened to destroy the "final" kingdom, the one comprised of feet and toes of iron and clay in Daniel 2.

Jesus had been telling those who would listen that rising against Roman oppression would bring nothing but their destruction. "Going the other mile" was about being forced to carry the Roman mailbag by soldiers for a mile. Rather than fighting it, just volunteer to help for another mile.

Who knows? You might make a Roman friend as you walk and chat with him. Have you ever wondered how Cornelius [Acts 10] or the unnamed Centurion [Matthew 8] got to be so friendly with the Jews? Don't resist the soldier who is gruff and slaps you on your cheek. Cheerfully offer the other. Or maybe just get out of his way. Don't resist the evil Roman. The life you save may be your own.

His message of the gospel, embodied in Jesus as King of the Kingdom of God, did not go over with the entrenched authorities, religious and secular.

It only resonated with the ordinary people, who were tired of their own political oppressors and hypocritical religious leaders. They were also tired of the Roman crackdowns that came every time some idiot zealot tried to kill a Roman soldier or official. Jesus, by his teaching and healing, appealed to them in ways that the entrenched secular and spiritual leadership could not.

Jesus goes on to fulfill the many messianic prophecies of the Old Testament by healing the blind and lame, and feeding multitudes with small amounts of bread and fish. He also proclaims God's instructions from a mountain like Moses, except that He claims the authority to tell the people to obey in mind and heart as well as body. He fulfills another prophecy by entering Jerusalem on a donkey (Zechariah 9:9, Matthew 21:5), and the people hail Him as their king.

It is said that no good deed goes unpunished. This is especially true in the case of Jesus. No matter who Jesus helps, the religious authorities try to find some way to spin it as a breaking of the law of Moses. At one point they even call him Beelzebub - literally the Devil. The one good deed that truly set their teeth on edge and drove them to murder was the raising of Lazarus from the dead.

Jesus had been teaching out-of-town for a number of days, and word reached him that his friend Lazarus, the brother of Mary and Martha Magdalene, was sick and seemed to be dying. Jesus tells his disciples that, even in death, all is not lost for his friend, and that God would be glorified. He continues teaching two more days, then returns to Bethany, home of his friends.

Mary and Martha are both disappointed that Jesus had not come in time to save Lazarus' life. They are in for a surprise, as Jesus has come to raise the four-day-dead man back to life. He does exactly that, literally commanding the dead man to come out of the tomb. As the bound man exits the tomb, the people around are shocked.

It was not so much that a man had been brought back to life. That had happened before in Israel with Elijah, for instance. Elijah had prayed over a young man and had brought him to life (1 Kings 17:7-24). Jesus even referred to that event when confronting the religious authorities in Luke 4:24-26.

It was more the manner in which Jesus did so. Not even Elijah had *commanded* a man to come back to life! Think about it. Do *you* know anyone who can just *order* a dead person to come back to life and walk out of the grave? Jesus is Lord over the living *and the dead.*

This is a level of authority on earth that is without precedent in human history.

When word was brought back to the authorities, they determined that if people followed Jesus after this "stunt" the Romans would destroy their nation and their privileged position under the Romans. The only way to stop him now was to kill him before everybody found out about his ability to raise the dead. And so the plotting began.

Judas Iscariot, one of Jesus' disciples, decides to turn Jesus over to the authorities and looks for an opportunity to do so. He is paid 30 pieces of silver to deliver Jesus to them. This fulfills a prophecy from Zechariah 11:12 about thirty pieces of silver, the "handsome price at which they valued me." (After Jesus' death Judas would commit suicide and be buried in the "potter's field," fulfilling the other part of the prophetic analogy)

Jesus has his disciples together for a Passover meal, but one day early, as He knew He would become the true Passover sacrifice for sin the following afternoon. (He couldn't very well have a Passover supper while buried in the grave.) After eating with the disciples and even having his feet washed by Jesus, Judas excuses himself from the meal and goes to betray Jesus to the priests.

After supper Jesus takes the disciples out to a nearby park, where Jesus prays and his disciples fall asleep. Judas arrives with a mob armed with clubs and betrays Jesus with a kiss. Peter cuts off the ear of one of the high priest's servants, but Jesus puts it back on and heals it, then tells the mob to let the disciples go. The disciples flee, but Peter and John hang back and follow the mob from a distance while they drag Jesus to the Sanhedrin, which is meeting illegally at night to try Jesus.

Not surprisingly, they find Jesus guilty of "blasphemy." Jesus claims to be the "Son of Man" who sits on "the right hand of the Mighty One" and who will come "on the clouds of heaven" (Matthew 26:64). Of course, it is only blasphemy if it is not true. If the reader of that story has not already established the truth of Jesus' identity as the Son of God by that point in the narrative he or she is unlikely to believe what follows either.

Jesus, who has been warning the Jews *not* to rebel against Rome during his entire ministry, is dragged to the judgment seat of Pontius Pilate, the Governor, on charges of *sedition against Rome.* Note that it is not what he has been charged with by the Sanhedrin, which was the charge of blasphemy.

Even after finding Jesus innocent of the charge of sedition, Pilate is coerced into having Jesus crucified by threats of violent demonstrations by the mob. Jesus is beaten and whipped by the Roman guards and forced to carry the crosspiece of his crucifix on the way to Golgotha for execution. The beating and whipping have so weakened him that he collapses on the way, and Simon of Cyrene is forced into carrying the crosspiece the rest of the way.

Once there, the real torture begins as they nail his hands and feet to the cross and jam the cross into place in its hole. At about noon the entire sky becomes dark, and the darkness lasts for three hours. This darkness is accompanied by an earthquake as Jesus breathes His last.

Some of the few who have not immediately dismissed this recorded period of darkness have claimed that it must have been an eclipse. Not only is three hours much longer than an eclipse, but this event was tied to the Passover which always happens in the middle of the lunar month. The lunar month starts at the new moon, which means that Passover *must* occur *during the full moon.* This is important because the full moon always occurs when the moon is *behind the earth relative to the sun.* There can never be a solar eclipse during Passover because the moon is on the wrong side of the earth.

This is not the only interesting fact about the three hours of darkness. The darkness was noticed as far away as Rome and captured in other historical documents. This was no local event. Three Graeco-Roman historians mention the event. Historian Thallus, though we no longer have his original work, is quoted by Julius Africanus as describing that darkness as an eclipse. Julius seems to doubt that the naturalistic explanation fits the event because he is aware of the moon's position at Passover. He is also aware that eclipses do not set off earthquakes, which he notes that Phlegon, another historian has also associated with this darkness.

Not only does Julius Africanus describe the darkness, but he also suggests that it was a global event, which accords with the writings of Christian writer Tertullian, who agrees that "the light departed from the sun, and the land was darkened at noonday, which wonder is related in your own annals, and is preserved in your archives to this day."

Phlegon, a Greek historian writing around 137 AD, even gives us a year and an exact time of day that matches the biblical account. He notes that it takes place in the fourth year of the 202nd Olympiad, which translates to 33 AD. He adds that "it became night in the sixth hour of the day [translation: noon] so that stars even appeared in the heavens. There was a great earthquake in Bithynia, and many things were overturned in Nicaea." So not only are are the darkness and the time it started consistent with the Gospels, he also mentions the earthquake (Matthew 27:51) that was felt as far away as Nicea in northwestern Asia Minor (now called Iznik in modern Turkey).

According to the eyewitnesses, Jesus died and was buried before sundown as the first holy day of the Feast of Unleavened Bread was about to begin. He rose from the dead before dawn on what we now call Sunday, which featured a biblical ritual of harvesting the first sheaf of new grain of the year and waving it before God, grinding it and cooking it on the Temple's altar as thanks to God for the harvest. Only after this ritual can the harvest officially begin.

In other words, Jesus is raised at the time of the offering of "first fruits" to God, as the "first fruits" of the resurrection. For anyone who has studied the festivals God commanded Israel at Mount Sinai, the connection could not be clearer. Jesus died as our Passover and is raised as the first fruits of the resurrection.

Recall from the story of Israel's crossing of the Red Sea that it took place overnight and that the Egyptian army was drowned at sunrise of the third day after Israel left Egypt the morning after the first Passover. God has the timing down exactly.

8

Jesus as Messiah

Jesus "Atones" For Human Sin

Some scholars and theologians claim that Jesus fulfills at least 300 prophecies. Since this includes His own death and resurrection this makes it extremely unlikely that Jesus would have been able to do so unless He is who He says He is.

In fact, the most important fulfillment is that of being "a prophet like Moses" from Deuteronomy 18:15. This passage is so important that the disciples of Jesus cite it in Acts 3:22 and 7:37 as they preach about Him. As Moses led people out of literal Egypt, Jesus leads people out of the spiritual Egypt of sin and death. How does Jesus do this? Another prophecy provides the clue that puts the puzzle together.

One of the strangest prophecies of all is from Isaiah 53:1-12. This indicates that the "servant of God" would suffer and die for the sins of the people. Somehow, after dying, this same person will be given "a portion among the great" and would "divide the spoils with the strong."

How do you divide the spoils once you have died? The answer is surprisingly simple: you come back to life. I did not say it was easy, just simple. How many people do *you* know who can pull that one off?

According to the Gospel writers, this is exactly what Jesus did. He was in the grave three days and three nights, then was seen by ten of His remaining eleven apostolic disciples on the Sunday evening after Passover. He was seen by the eleventh the following Sunday. They all saw the wounds in His side and hands, and presumably His feet (He wore sandals, after all). They were all convinced that Jesus had come back to life after being dead for three days. There is more to say about that later.

Strangely enough, Isaiah 53 does not seem to be a part of the normal synagogue scripture reading cycle. The Isaiah 53 passage is puzzling even to modern Jewish scholars, who certainly do not want to apply it to a Christian Messiah, let alone Jesus of Nazareth. It seems to me that trying to hide the passage from your people suggests that there is no other better explanation than its fulfillment by Jesus.

Just as Israel crossed the Red Sea on the third day after Passover, Jesus passed from death to life on the third day after the Passover on which He died. Not coincidentally, a sheaf of the very first grain of the year was offered as a "wave offering" at that very moment, symbolizing God's acceptance of the "first-fruits" of the harvest. This was always done on the first day of the week during the week of unleavened bread, usually referred to as Passover week. This was also the first day of the countdown to the feast of Pentecost.

What I am saying by the previous paragraph is that God had this planned from the very beginning. It happened at exactly the right time, in the right year, and on the right day. God planned Jesus' death to happen on Passover and His resurrection to happen on a Sunday during Passover week that corresponded to the third day after Passover so that Jesus could fulfil the analogy of crossing the "Red Sea" of death while also being the "first-fruits" of the resurrection (1 Corinthians 15:20-23).

Not surprisingly, science cannot explain how someone can be dead for several days, and then come back to life. Their response is to deny the possibility as scientifically impossible. Of course these are people alive almost 2000 years after the death and resurrection of Jesus who try to deny it ever happened. They casually dismiss the fact that all of the eyewitnesses refused to recant of promoting his resurrection as a real historical event. Almost all were killed for refusing to deny Jesus as their resurrected God.

(None denied His resurrection or His being God, but John did survive to a ripe old age.)

The scientific irony is truly rich if you consider that unguided evolution from non-living matter into living being is theoretically even less likely than reanimating formerly living matter. At least the dead have the chemical components already present in their systems, Scientists can believe that humans can evolve from non-living matter without any intelligent design, but the same ones can't believe that a man can be raised from the dead by the intelligent and all-powerful God who created the universe and all living creatures.

I should get back to the question of how Jesus leads His people out of "Egypt." To do so we need to remember the story of Abraham walking three days to Mount Moriah to sacrifice his son Isaac. God had promised that Isaac would be the son who would father a great nation for Abraham. God also asked Abraham to sacrifice Isaac to Him. Humanly speaking, this is an impossible situation. How can a dead, childless youth father a great nation?

As I mentioned before, the writer of the book of Hebrews infers something from Abraham's words to the servant who would stay at the foot of the mountain. Abraham tells him that both he and his son would come back to them after the sacrifice (Genesis 22:5). From this the writer of Hebrews concludes that Abraham reasoned that God can even raise the dead (Hebrews 11:19). That is certainly a logical conclusion if you believe that God made the first man out of dust of the ground and breathed life into him.

How is it that Isaac returns with Abraham? God relents and provides a substitute sacrifice, a ram caught in a thicket. Substitution is the key. God offers His own Son as a substitute for the penalty of our sin: death. It only makes logical sense that the life of the Life-Giver is "worth" more than the sum of the lives He created. God has proven that He is willing to give up the very thing He asked Abraham to give up. He gave up His Son as a substitute to die on our behalf, enabling our salvation.

Jesus versus Sin and Death

To be clear, the "Egypt" that Jesus leads His people out of is both sin and death. The Bible speaks of, death as the result of sin (see Romans 5:12 and 6:23), and is therefore the root cause of death. To defeat death requires the defeat of sin.

So how do you defeat sin? In a sense, it is the same way that Jesus defeats the power of the Jewish religious establishment as well as the might of Rome. You let them do their worst, then come back, alive, even after they have killed you. Once you have paid the penalty for the crime, you go free. The problem is that death *is the penalty* of sin. The only way out is to die and then be resurrected, just like Jesus promises, if you faithfully follow Him until that first death.

> *Hebrews 9:27-28 KJV And as it is appointed unto men once to die, but after this the judgment: So Christ was once offered to bear the sins of many; and unto them that look for him shall he appear *the second time without sin unto salvation.*

There is a judgment that every human being must undergo. Those who follow Jesus look forward to that judgment, for Jesus "appears" to bring them "salvation" from a verdict of "guilty." This is why Revelation 20: 6 speaks of how those involved in the "first resurrection" (at Jesus' return to earth) do not partake of the "second death." On the other hand, those whose names are not found inscribed in the "book of life" are cast into a "lake of fire," into which, oddly enough, "death and hell [hades]" are also cast. More about this last part later in this book.

Jesus tells Peter that the "gates of hell" cannot prevail over His church. Nobody in military history has ever attacked an enemy with a "gate." Gates are a part of a *defensive* fortification. In reality "hell" is akin to being a "prison" of the dead. Jesus is saying that each life He saves is one that is broken out of hell. The gates are broken and the prisoners can go free.

Psalm 68 describes God arriving in a royal procession. It is quite the spectacle. God "rides on the clouds" and He "leads out the prisoners with singing." The Apostle Paul uses verse 18, "When you ascended on high, you took many captives; you received gifts from people, even from the rebellious" as an analogy of how Jesus saves (Ephesians 4:8). Jesus saves by releasing prisoners and taking them to His capitol in His train.

In other words, He brings them to be His own servants, and they follow Him. We are freed *from* sin, not freed *to* sin. Paul writes, "Do you not know that your bodies are temples of the Holy Spirit, who is in you, whom you have received from God? You are not your own; you were bought at a price. Therefore, honor God with your bodies."

The price God paid is the death of His Son. When we accept that sacrifice, we accept Jesus as our Lord and God, just as "doubting Thomas" did in John 20:28 when he saw the resurrected Jesus and believed. Thomas literally calls him, "My Lord and my God!" When you are "bought" you become the property of the one who bought you.

Here is the question that each person who reads the Bible eventually must face. Is it better to be bought by God or remain a slave to sin and death? If living forever, never knowing sadness again, no longer fearing death or loss, and living in a city "whose architect and builder is God" sound like great working conditions, the answer is obvious.

This is good news! The four books that describe the life and ministry of Jesus in the Bible are called "Gospels," which comes from an older English word that literally means "good news."

Jesus and Baptizing with the Holy Spirit

Did you notice what Paul also says about the bodies of followers of Jesus? What is this about being "temples of the Holy Spirit?" What or who is the Holy Spirit?

We were introduced to the Holy Spirit in this particular book as the means by which Mary becomes pregnant with Jesus. In the Bible, however, the Holy Spirit has a long and storied role. We find the "Spirit of God" hovering over the newly created ball of water that would become the world and universe that we know today (Genesis 1:2). Prior to the Flood, in Genesis 6:3 we find that God's Spirit has been contending with humans, and would continue to do so even with a reduction in the human lifespan.

When Egypt's Pharaoh hears Joseph's wisdom, he discerns that Joseph has the "spirit of God" in him (Genesis 41:38). Once Israel is at Mount Sinai God fills certain artisans with His Spirit to give them knowledge and skill to construct and supervise construction of His Tabernacle.

In Numbers 11 Moses complains that the burden of leading all of the people of Israel is too heavy for one man, God takes "some of the power of the Spirit that was on him [Moses] and put it on the seventy elders." At that moment the elders begin to "prophesy." This links the Spirit of God to all forms of prophetic ministry in the Old Testament, including Moses himself as the archetype of Old Testament prophetic ministry. Moses even wishes that all of God's people had His Spirit and were therefore prophets. That leads us to Jesus and what happens both on the night before His death and the day of Pentecost.

As John the Baptist explains to his audience, "the one on whom you see the Spirit come down and remain is the one who will baptize with the Holy Spirit" (John 1:33). He had seen the Holy Spirit descend, appearing as a dove, and land on Jesus (v. 32). Matthew, Mark and Luke also record the event. Jesus is therefore the one that John the Baptist claims would "baptize" with the Holy Spirit.

Jesus proclaims His mission in the synagogue in Nazareth in Luke 4:14-21. He begins the sermon by reading a passage from Isaiah 61:1. He begins by confirming that John was correct about the Spirit of God being on Him.

> *"The Spirit of the Lord is on me, because he has anointed me to proclaim good news to the poor. He has sent me to proclaim freedom for the prisoners and recovery of sight for the blind, to set the oppressed free, to proclaim the year of the Lord's favor." Then he rolled up the scroll, gave it back to the attendant and sat down.*

> *The eyes of everyone in the synagogue were fastened on him. He began by saying to them, Today this scripture is fulfilled in your hearing."*

In John 3 Jesus is approached at night by a leading Pharisee, Nicodemus. Jesus tells Nicodemus that he must be "born again." After Nicodemus wonders about re-entering a mother's womb, Jesus replies that nobody "can enter the Kingdom of God unless they are born of water and the Spirit."

Just in case we wonder about being "born of water," John's disciples come with a complaint that Jesus is moving in on John's ministry by baptizing people too. It seems that the one step in being "born again" is water baptism. But what about "baptism with the Holy Spirit" and being "born again?"

It turns out that prophets had been telling us about it centuries before Jesus. Remember Moses wishing that all of God's people could be prophets by having the Lord's Spirit? How did John the Baptist know about Jesus and the Holy Spirit? Isaiah wrote in Isaiah 11:1-2 that a "root" and "branch" of Jesse would have the Spirit of the Lord resting on Him. You can only be both a root and a branch if you are both Jesse's ancestor and his descendant. Jesus was both, as God in the flesh. As the Word, He made Adam out of the dust of the ground, becoming Adam's "father" because Adam is made in God's image (as a baby is made in the image of its parents).

Ezekiel speaks of a time when God puts a "new spirit" or "my Spirit" in the hearts of the people of Israel. He says so repeatedly, as in 11:19, 36:26-27 and 39:29. Most shockingly of all, if you take it literally, He even promises to put His Spirit into Israel *after they have died* and are *brought back to life* in 37:12-14. Read it for yourself and let the implications sink in. I will reflect more about the possibilities toward the end of this book.

The prophet Joel speaks of a time when God will pour out His Spirit "on all people." This includes both men and women, slave and free (Joel 2:28-29). Peter quotes that passage to explain what has happened on the day of Pentecost to the disciples of Jesus in Acts 2. More on that later.

On Jesus' last night with the disciples before His death on Passover day Jesus tells them that He will send an "Advocate," but only after Jesus "goes (dies)" (John 16:7). Also known as the Spirit of Truth, he will guide the disciples into all truth, glorify Jesus and enable them to testify about Him (John 15:26-27, 16:13-15).

As darkness was descending on the day Jesus had been resurrected His disciples were gathered in a locked room. Jesus appears, shocking them. After showing them that He is real by displaying the wounds in his hands and side He tells them "As the Father has sent me, I am sending you." He then *breathes on them* and says, "Receive the Holy Spirit."

If you have been reading and understanding the Bible, this should remind you of God breathing the "breath of life" into Adam at his creation. Jesus is breathing new life into His disciples, transitioning them from "fleshly" life to "spiritual" life (John 20:19-23). This new "spiritual life" would become highly visible ("manifest") to the Jewish community on the day of Pentecost, seven weeks later.

Notice also that the context of their receiving of the Spirit is that Jesus is sending them "as the Father has sent" Jesus. If Jesus has been sent to "baptize with the Holy Spirit," is He also sending the disciples to do the same thing? Can the disciples baptize with the Holy Spirit?

In Acts 8 we read that the church is being persecuted and scattered. Philip the deacon finds himself in a city in Samaria. Now Samaritans had their own version of the Jewish Temple, and could be considered a sort of Jewish heretical cult. Since Jesus had previously preached in Samaria it seemed like a good place to continue ministry. He preaches about Jesus the Messiah there, performing signs and driving out demons. Crowds gather and people believe and are baptized, but the Holy Spirit does not enter them. Peter and John find out about these believers, notice that they do not yet have the Holy Spirit and place their hands on them. As they place hands upon them, the Holy Spirit enters these new believers in visible ways.

In an aside, we find a sorcerer named Simon who is amazed by Philip's miracle-working and becomes a believer and baptized. He sees Peter and John laying hands on people and receiving the Spirit. He approaches them and offers them money to acquire this ability himself.

Notice that he, a sorcerer by trade, does not ask Philip for the power to drive out demons. Somehow, the gift of baptizing by the Spirit is even more amazing to this former sorcerer than driving out demons. This is the "power" that he wants for himself. It does not take a rocket scientist to figure out that this is not right, and Peter tells him that he has "no share in this ministry" (8:22-23). This is the biblical equivalent of telling him to "take a hike."

This side-story establishes that the apostles not only can provide the baptism of the Holy Spirit, but that they can also deny it to the unsuitable. We see how the disciples can either forgive sins or deny forgiveness of sins, such as in the case of Simon the sorcerer. Peter sees a man who is captive to sin, and simply warns him rather than baptizing him with the Holy Spirit. Every word of Jesus to and about His disciples is coming true according to these accounts.

Luke tells us in Acts 10 that Peter baptizes the first Gentile converts, Cornelius the centurion and all of his family. For the Jewish Christian community this comes as a shock, since they are expecting only descendants of Abraham to be accepted by God. "While Peter was still speaking these words, the Holy Spirit came on all who heard the message" (vs. 44) How do Peter and those who came with him know? These Gentiles who believed began speaking with the same "tongues" as Peter and the original 120 disciples did (vs.46). Peter concludes that they should be baptized in water, since their baptism of the Spirit had occurred already, just from hearing and believing the gospel as spoken by Peter.

As Peter was explaining this to some critical believers in Jerusalem he explains, "Then I remembered what the Lord had said: 'John baptized with water, but you will be baptized with the Holy Spirit.' So if God gave them the same gift he gave us who believed in the Lord Jesus Christ, who was I to think that I could stand in God's way?" Once Peter says this, all of the objections disappeared, and they began to praise God together.

So now Moses belatedly gets his wish that all of God's people could have the same Spirit that he did, and Joel's prophecy about the same thing begins to be fulfilled in Jesus' disciples. The torch of baptism of the Holy Spirit is passed on through Jesus' disciples.

9

Jesus on the Heavenly Throne

What Is Jesus Doing Now?

Going back to the end of Luke's Gospel, we read, "When he had led them out to the vicinity of Bethany, he lifted up his hands and blessed them. While he was blessing them, he left them and was taken up into heaven. Then they worshiped him and returned to Jerusalem with great joy."

Jesus leaves the disciples by rising into the air and is taken to heaven. Notice that the disciples are actually *worshiping* Jesus, suggesting that they are acknowledging that He is God in the flesh. This definitely goes against the modern notion that later believers imbued him with supernatural characteristics well after the death of the original disciples.

Some modern writers have tried to make a distinction between the "Jesus of history" and the "Jesus of faith." The idea is that Jesus was just a man whose legend grew into a myth as the story was told throughout the generations. Yet, reading the Gospels, one cannot but have the impression that Jesus' disciples understood that this Jesus who lived among them was exactly who He said He was, the Son of God. Jesus is the Jesus of both history and faith, since He is both God and human.

Jesus had told them that he had come from the Father in heaven and was going back to the Father. He had told them that He would be persecuted, die and come back to life after three days. They witnessed that He died and came back to life. They then saw him rise into the sky, presumably to heaven.

Since nobody had ever flown before, they saw His rising as confirmation that He was going back to His Father.

Jesus had told them to wait in Jerusalem until God provides them with "power from on high. This happened on day of Pentecost, which is the Greek name for the biblical "feast of weeks" or "feast of harvest." Once the Holy Spirit manifested in the 120 gathered in the upper room, the message of Jesus as Messiah spread like wildfire.

At this point it seems as though the Holy Spirit has taken over, and Jesus is nowhere to be found. Or is He? Well, we assume that Jesus is with His Father, but what is He doing up there? Is Jesus experiencing early retirement? Or is Jesus working on other aspects of His Messianic occupation, like working with His church and with the people of Israel? Fortunately for us, the New Testament writers provide us with pieces of that puzzle.

Jesus Works With Saul of Tarsus

For instance, in Acts 9, as Saul of Tarsus is on his way to Damascus to capture and persecute Christians, he is met by a bright light and falls to the ground, blinded. A voice asks Saul why he is persecuting the speaker. When Saul asks who is speaking, Jesus identifies Himself, then tells Saul what to do. Jesus then addresses a disciple named Ananias and tells him to find Saul and restore Saul's sight by placing his hands on him.

Paul later tells the church in Galatia that he received the gospel he preached directly from Jesus Christ, and that he first met some of the original disciples of Jesus only after spending three years isolated from them in Arabia (Galatians 1:11-20). We discover in 4:25 in the same letter, as noted before, that Arabia is also the place where Mount Sinai is located. We can then suspect that Saul, renamed Paul, learned the gospel under the direct tutelage of Jesus in the region of Mount Sinai, the same place as God pronounced His covenant with Israel centuries before. There could be no more appropriate place for that schooling.

So we have Jesus actively intervening in the life and ministry of the Apostle Paul some time after His ascension to heaven. He is clearly still engaged with His people to at least some degree. Is there more?

Jesus is Head Of the Church

There is an even more striking way that Jesus continues to work in the church throughout the ages. Paul notes in Romans 8:9-10 that true believers in Jesus not only have the Holy Spirit in them, but that this same Spirit is even known as the Spirit of Christ. He goes on to say that if you do not have the "Spirit of Christ" you do not belong to Christ. "But if Christ is in you, then even though your body is subject to death because of sin, the Spirit gives life because of righteousness."

To recap, the Spirit of God, promised in the Old Testament, actually puts Jesus Christ's Spirit into each true believer, enabling the believer to belong to Christ and be imbued with Christ's "righteousness." This enables the believer to be resurrected to life after he or she has died. So, what does having the "Spirit of Christ" in us have to do with Jesus ruling the church in this present time?

I'll use an analogy from modern diplomacy. A nation usually has embassies or consulates located in countries with which they have diplomatic relations. The embassy or consulate must stay up-to-date with laws, regulations and policies of their home country while being aware of the local laws and regulations. In order to stay up-to-date, some form of communication system must be active for sending messages back and forth with the homeland.

Diplomats working at these outposts of their homeland also send messages from their homeland to the powers-that-be in their host country. Sometimes these messages are complimentary, but often they are not. Their homeland may want to let the host country know that something they have done or are doing is morally or legally wrong. In extreme cases diplomats may be asked to return to their home country as a warning that their country has gone too far, and their homeland refuses to communicate any further.

At other times the embassy receives messages from the host government in the same vein, either complimentary or critical. In extreme cases, ambassadors may even be expelled from a country or embassies and consulates closed.

Christians have a "citizenship" in heaven. As such we are each representatives of what can be considered a "foreign" government, the Kingdom of God. The Spirit of Christ allows instantaneous communication with the King, Jesus Christ, because His Spirit is within each Christian. We pray to inform Jesus of our needs as well as the needs of any who wish to acquire heavenly citizenship and join us.

As an aside, this is the root reason that Christianity is the most persecuted religion, (except for Judaism, for reasons discussed earlier) in the world. Christians, because of the Spirit of Christ, tend to act and speak in ways that contradict the normal ways that nations operate. This is a normal consequence of Jesus' prophetic occupation of calling out evil and oppression within his own people. That is why they killed Jesus.

This is the main difference between an ambassador and a Christian. The Kingdom of God is not generally recognized by this world's national governments or international organizations of governments. With very few exceptions in history, Christians have had no diplomatic immunity, and tend to be summarily dismissed, jailed, beaten or killed when their "host" nation or citizenry does not want to hear Jesus' message to them. This can even happen within theoretically "Christian" nations when power structures have ossified in totalitarian directions. This is why wars have occurred between "Christian" nations, as Jesus' message is increasingly ignored by one side, the other, or both.

I will note in passing that religion is neither the main cause of war nor even a secondary cause of most wars. While it is certainly true that evil leaders use religion as a motivation to war, it is actually the twisted, greedy nature of some human beings that is at the root of war. James writes in 4:1-3 that fights and quarrels arise from selfish desires and illicit wants that lead to violence. Even within the second generation of mankind jealousy led to murder (Genesis 4:1-16). Real Christians see war as a last resort, and only when there is a need to defend the country or defend the helpless.

Remember that even Saul of Tarsus, who became the Apostle to the Gentiles as Paul, was originally on the "get rid of the Christians" team. He understood the psychology of that in very deep ways as he presented Jesus' gospel to Jew and Gentile alike. As a convert to Jesus, he could compare the riches of the Spirit of Christ with the cost of losing everything he had striven for in his previous life. He even states, "What is more, I consider everything a loss because of the surpassing worth of knowing Christ Jesus my Lord, for whose sake I have lost all things. I consider them garbage, that I may gain Christ."

Jesus Is Mediator Between God and Humanity

The writer of Hebrews shows another way Jesus is active in the world, even though He is in heaven.

> *For the [W]ord of God is living and active, sharper than any two-edged sword, piercing to the division of soul and of spirit, of joints and of marrow, and discerning the thoughts and intentions of the heart. (Hebrews 4:12 - KJV)*

> *Nothing in all creation is hidden from God's sight. Everything is uncovered and laid bare before the eyes of him to whom we must give account. Therefore, since we have a great high priest who has ascended into heaven, Jesus the Son of God, let us hold firmly to the faith we profess. For we do not have a high priest who is unable to empathize with our weaknesses, but we have one who has been tempted in every way, just as we are—yet he did not sin. Let us then approach God's throne of grace with confidence, so that we may receive mercy and find grace to help us in our time of need. (Hebrews 4:13-16 - NIV)*

You may have noticed the change in the translation I used between verses 12 and 13 above. In verse 12 the King James Version is closer to the Greek grammar of the original, and I use it because it makes more sense to understand "the word" as "the Word," referring to Jesus as verse 12 moves into verse 13. Otherwise the subject of verse 12 becomes different than "God" in verse 13. If "the word" refers to the pages of the Bible, as many believe, why does it "discern the thoughts and intentions of the heart?" It makes more sense if "the Word" is God, who discerns and before whose eyes "everything is uncovered and laid bare."

The rest of the passage explains what Jesus is doing for Christians during this time before His promised return. Jesus is our High Priest, whom we can approach on God's throne for mercy and "grace to help in our time of need."

Part of that last sentence is obvious. Even as Christians we are prone to screwing up, which is why we need mercy. Repentance is not a one-time deal. Repentance involves noticing when we are engaging in anti-Christian activity and thinking, acknowledging the problem to Christ, asking forgiveness, then changing our thinking and actions to bring them into alignment with Jesus' values. The key is that Jesus is available to hear our confession and forgive.

However, there is more to it than just mercy. Where does the ability to change our thinking and actions come from? That is where "grace to help" comes in. We are in a constant conflict within ourselves between Christ's Spirit in us and the natural desires of our baser nature. "Grace" is a word that comes from the idea of "a gift." In the context of that verse it refers to a supernatural gift that enables a Christian to overcome normal human temptations in order to do the right thing in God's eyes.

Speaking to this same issue to the church in Philippi, Paul writes, "for it is God who works in you to will and to act in order to fulfill his good purpose" (Philippians 2:13). Grace is actually God working in us through His Spirit to motivate both the desire to do the right thing and the acting on that desire - the actual doing.

If anyone knows how to resist temptation in order to do the right thing it is surely Jesus Christ. He can grant us that gift if we go to Him and ask for it in our "time of need."

So far, we have seen Jesus literally working to train a new apostle, live in and communicate with Christians in an ambassadorial/prophetic role to the world, and work in God's headquarters as High Priest to intercede for and provide spiritual strength to His people. Is there anything else Jesus does in His copious spare time?

Jesus is the Active Lord of Heaven and Earth

There is more, much more. Jesus is ruler over all, according to Paul in Ephesians 1:21-23. This includes all of the kingdoms of the earth and even the spiritual forces behind the scenes that influence all nations. They can only do what Jesus allows them or orders them to do. Later on, I will address the implications of this for evil in the world in terms of why a good God allows evil.

For now, I defer to Paul's take that Jesus is Lord of heaven and earth, as revealed by Jesus Himself to Paul during his three years in Arabia. Paul also notes in the verses above that Jesus is currently the Head of the church. Even though He is in heaven, He does not have a passive role, as noted above in His dealings with Paul.

In addressing the Athenian city council Paul states in Acts 17:28 that their "unknown god" is the true God and that "in him we live and move and have our being." Combine this with Paul's statement in verses 30 and 31 that God commands all people everywhere to repent and that Jesus, "the man he has appointed" will judge the world with justice, and you have an active God who is aware of all living beings and will judge appropriately. In Rev. 4:11 John uses similar language that all humans "have their being" in the man seated on God's throne, Jesus.

Paul goes even further Colossians 1:15-17. Not only did the Son create everything in the universe, including thrones, powers or rulers or authorities, but this was all created "through him and for him." In the present Jesus is the one in whom "all things hold together." Not only is Jesus in charge, He is the one who sustains it all.

The job description of Jesus the Son of God is not one to be taken on lightly. Jesus appears to be the absolutely ultimate multi-tasker. However, in the words of the late-night infomercial, "but wait, there's more."

Jesus Is the Active Judge of the World and the Church

Jesus is currently watching members of His church and judging them as they live their lives. In 1 Corinthians 11:27-32 Paul addresses a particular problem the church faces as they show favoritism among themselves at what is called "the Lord's supper" or "communion." Those who do not treat other members of the church with proper human dignity and respect or who withhold needed help are being watched by Jesus. Paul notes that this has led to weakness, sickness and even death among believers as a judgment from Christ.

He then tells them that they can avoid these negative judgments by first judging themselves and living rightly with each other. Nevertheless, Paul also points out that even the negative consequences are actually a form of discipline intended to prevent a much harsher condemnation that will eventually befall the world. In other words, Jesus saving the righteous is an active process that even involves discipline to keep the believer on the right course.

In speaking of judgment and salvation, Peter also lets a group of churches know that Jesus both saves and judges. In 2 Peter 2:4--9 he speaks of several Old Testament judgments, such as the global flood and the "firing" of Sodom and Gomorrah as examples of how God saved certain righteous people from them. He goes on to say that Christ knows how to both save the righteous and "hold the unrighteous for punishment on the day of judgment." This suggests that Jesus knows who the unrighteous are who deserve final punishment, and that He somehow "holds" them until that time. There will be more about the "hold" later in this book.

The writer of Hebrews seems to agree with Paul and Peter, because in Hebrews 4:12-13 he writes that "nothing in Creation" is hidden from God's sight. God is identified as "the [W]ord of God in verse 12, as I noted earlier. He is the one to whom everyone must "give account." The context is that people might "perish" because of "disobedience" if they do not make the effort to "enter the rest" of God.

So far the above has been mostly targeted to the church, though there were warnings about avoiding the judgment on the world. Jesus is also actively judging the world. In fact, much of the book of Revelation describes the judgments on the world in an effort to persuade Christians not to abandon Jesus in the face of persecution.

Jesus and Judgment in the Book of Revelation

The book of Revelation describes what looks like at least two competing world superpowers. (A comparison with some parts of the book of Daniel would seem to suggest three, as two from the north and east seem to converge on a revived Roman Empire that has reoccupied Jerusalem.)

There is also what appears to be a religious power ruling over the nations of the revived Roman empire. This main religious villain is described as "Babylon the Great," which appears to be situated on seven hills. This of course suggests the city of Rome, though it could be symbolic of any system that dominates in the way the Babylonian Mystery religion did, by means of crafty and deceitful "miracles."

A major problem with Babylon the Great is the persecution of all Christians within its territory, so one may conclude that Babylon the Great is a major politico-religious entity devoted to crushing Christianity. Jesus promises to avenge the blood of His people on Babylon the Great. He begins by sending plague after plague upon this unholy alliance of God-hating peoples. Forests and croplands burn, water turns to blood, massive hailstorms with fire and earthquakes cause massive upheaval, yet people still do not repent.

God judges, and allows "Babylon the Great" to be destroyed as though it had been dropped into the sea. This happens when the European superpower turns on its "rider" in favor of a man (probably demonically possessed) who thinks of himself as a god.

The military might of Europe seems at first to be impossible to defeat. However, like Napoleon and Hitler before it, aggressive hubris becomes the cause of its undoing. Europe attempts to take on more territory than it can handle. This causes the nations of the north and east converge on Jerusalem, initially to make war on the European superpower.

Behind the scenes, we see that they are instigated by three demons that look like frogs emanating from the mouths of "the dragon," "the beast" and "the false prophet." Just as they begin to engage in combat, they see Jesus arriving in the clouds and instead attempt to attack Him. The attempt will fail in spectacular fashion.

Even further behind the scenes we learn that Jesus was actually drawing out all of the military might of the world to His earthly headquarters in order to take them all out at once. He supernaturally destroys all three armies, literally disarming all opposition and proving to the world that He cannot be defeated. This is the first part of judgment: judgment of the nations. He throws "the beast" and "the false prophet," still alive, into a fiery lake, yet the rest of the soldiers are simply "killed with the sword."

The "dragon, the ancient serpent, who is the devil, or Satan" is thrown into an abyss, which is locked and sealed to prevent his escape. He is locked up for 1000 years, then released in order to deceive the nations one final time before his final judgment. After his post-millennial armed rebellion is destroyed, he is cast into the same lake of fire as his two previous associates, the beast and the false prophet had been, and the three are to be tormented forever.

This leads to the final judgment on all humanity. Every human who had not been resurrected at Jesus' return are brought back to life before the throne of God to be judged. We are not told how long this takes. Books are opened, and another called "the book of life." We are not told how many are found in the book of life. All we are told is that those not found in it were thrown into the lake of fire. We are also told that death and Hades are thrown into the lake of fire, and that the lake of fire is the "second death."

The vast majority of Christians have been taught that those thrown into the fire will suffer endless torment forever, because that is what has been said of the beast, false prophet and the devil. I note that the unholy trinity seem to have demonic characteristics and are able to launch demons from their mouths, suggesting that they are in fact fallen angels.

We are not told that the human beings thrown into the lake are 1) alive when they are thrown in or 2) that they suffer forever. Those may or may not be the case, but those are *assumptions,* not stated facts.

We are also not told that everyone who has not heard of Christ is automatically condemned to the lake of fire. The reason I say this is because of the peculiar conditions described in Ezekiel 37:1-14. God gives "all the people of Israel" who had just been brought back to life in this "valley of dry bones" His Spirit in order that they may know that He is their Lord.

These people had long been dead in sin, as depicted by their state of non-burial. (In Israel, the greatest indignity you could offer to a hated criminal was to deny them proper burial.) They apparently did not know the God of Israel, yet God gives them the opportunity to know Him, post-mortem. Otherwise, why give them His Spirit so that they would know Him?

We should be cautious in describing the fate of all human beings in the Great Judgement when we do not have all of the information at our disposal. We need to make sure we teach truth and not speculation, especially speculation that makes God look like an uncaring monster who beats up on people who don't know Him.

Yes, Christians can and *should* **warn** people about God's Judgement Day. We need to remember, however, that we are not the Judge. God knows more about each person than we do. Judgement, in God's eyes, is a multifaceted and far-reaching enterprise.

For instance, He once appointed leaders and deliverers in Israel's early history, and called them "judges" rather than kings or priests. Some of these "judges" were military leaders, while others were priests or prophets, or even one who was not a natural leader, but a very strong man who could defeat a thousand armed enemy soldiers with the jawbone of a donkey. Read the book of Judges to find out more. You might be surprised at who God can work with to accomplish His goals.

While "the fear of the LORD is the beginning of wisdom" (Proverbs 1:7), we must also realize that "knowledge of the Holy One is understanding" (Proverbs 9:10). God is far wiser and more just than any human being, so we had better be careful not to underestimate Him nor substitute speculation for what God actually says or chooses not to tell us.

As a example of limits to our understanding of how God deals with humanity, we find the Apostle Paul writing, "For as in Adam all die, so in Christ shall all be made alive." Ask yourself this question: Is the "all" who die the same as the "all" who are made alive?

Do you actually **know** the answer, or are you just taking some expert's word for it?

Whatever the answer is, we know that Jesus Christ is the only one who can make the dead come alive.

10

Jesus and the Problem of Evil

Since we are on the subject of judgement we can come back to the problem of why, if God is so good, there is so much evil and suffering in the world.

By now you have figured out that I am what some have called a biblical literalist. In other words, if it is not obviously a poetic passage or an analogy or a figure of speech, I take what is said in the Bible literally. Many people don't like to make waves or don't care to contradict scientific consensus, but I stand by what is clearly stated in the Bible. This means that if the Bible has an explanation for the suffering and evil in the world, I want to know what it is.

Scientists and theologians have one thing in common. They tend to like using big words or jargon to describe how they see reality. I have read enough science and theology to have a decent understanding of many of the big words scientists use and most that theologians use, so they don't frighten me.

In a nutshell, the problem of evil and suffering boils down to human beings having a nature that is a mixture of good and evil. In the famous words of Aleksandr Solzhenitsyn from *The Gulag Archipelago*,

> *The line separating good and evil passes not through states, nor between classes, nor between political parties either – but right through every human heart...even within hearts overwhelmed by evil, one small bridgehead of good is retained. And even in the best of all hearts, there remains...an uprooted small corner of evil.*

Solzhenitsyn's insight is a powerful one that explains a lot of the malignancy and suffering in the world.

How human nature came to be a mixture of good and evil is actually explained early in the Bible, in Genesis 3. It starts with the conversation between the serpent and Eve. The serpent begins by twisting God's instruction about the tree of the knowledge of good and evil. He tells a lie followed by a half-truth. The bald lie is that they would not die. It took centuries, but they did die, and so has every human being ever since.

The half-truth is where our insight about current human nature comes in. Until that conversation, both Adam and Eve were happy to trust God to give them guidance to follow. Once the seed of distrust of God was sown by the serpent, both humans decided to take what was forbidden. Suddenly, they realize that they are "naked" and try to cover themselves out of shame. Out of the same shame, they try to hide from God. When confronted, they do what almost all children of a certain age do, shift blame.

When reading over that account I cannot help but notice that their response to God's questions reflect exactly what my own feelings are when I do something I know is wrong. Guilt, shame and hiding are natural responses that occur in almost all human beings who are not complete psychopaths. Was it some "secret ingredient" in the fruit of that tree that somehow infiltrated itself into the soul of every human being to taint our nature? Some contend that there is a "genetic" component of what is called "original sin" in every human being that warps our character.

I have never liked the idea of inheriting a sinful nature. That makes it sound like the game is rigged against every human being in terms of final judgment. As a young man I conceived of human sinfulness as learned behaviour picked up from the environment - parents, peers and society. I was not the first to think of that, by a long-shot. A monk named Pelagius came up with a formal theory to that effect in the early 400's AD. He strongly emphasized the idea of free human will. He theorized that God created each individual soul, so it must begin in an untainted state.

Unfortunately there is a problem with that idea. If humans start with a blank slate morally, where does evil come from? How and when do babies become selfish teenagers? Why do children have to be trained to control their aggressive impulses to properly socialize with other children by the age of four? And why are some children difficult to manage even from birth?

Why do all efforts to create a utopian society inevitably fail? It all comes down to an innate inability to completely control the self-centered aspect of our character. Every human being has a self-justifying psyche that wants to determine for itself what it considers good and evil. To whatever large or small degree, we want to make our own rules.

I remember watching a movie version of H.G. Welles' *The Shape of Things to Come.* What I found interesting later in the movie was the idea that you could completely control the mindset of a population by a program of indoctrination, to the point of curing corruption and selfishness. Even though I was a teenager I intuitively saw how ridiculous the notion was that education and indoctrination would eliminate the need for police or deterrence of crime by punishment. I wish to enter into the record in defence of my assessment the two socialist paradises of the Soviet Union and Maoist People's Republic of China. Their efforts to condition their populations to accept collectivist thinking resulted in the deaths of at least 100 million of their citizens.

Let us also not forget that the Nazi regime's official party name, *Nationalsozialistische deutsche Arbeiterpartei,* translates to "German National Socialist Workers' Party". Two of the four adjectives in their official name suggest that it was a left-wing rather than right-wing party. In other words it was a nationalist socialist party instead of an internationalist socialist party. The main difference is the racial targeting of which of their citizens they put to death.

All I had to do was watch my teenage classmates make decisions that harmed others or themselves to understand that there is something in our makeup that is irrational. When I turned my attention to my own actions, I could see their irrational thinking reflected in my own. It was my good fortune that I was a rather bookish and low-energy teen, which kept me out of much of the trouble my contemporaries got themselves into. It is not easy to get into a lot of trouble when you hang out in the library most of the time.

Of course, in an age of "scientific enlightenment" it is not possible to consider an additional reason that utopia is impossible in this world. The problem is that science, as practiced in the past two centuries, can say nothing about causes and effects that are not physical in nature. By and large, modern science denies the existence of the spiritual and the spirit world.

It is one thing to say that scientific endeavor is not able to measure or quantify anything that is not physical. That is certainly a true statement. It is another thing entirely for a scientist to claim that the non-material is not real. That statement itself is not falsifiable and cannot be scientifically verified.

The problem of evil is compounded by the outside influence of powerful but twisted non-human intelligences that the Bible describes as "demons," "devils," "Satan," or "spiritual wickedness in high places" (Ephesians 6:12). Science has nothing to say about these because they are not physical entities, but rather spiritual beings who inhabit a spiritual realm. That realm overlaps with ours but is not discernible to our physical senses.

William Shakespeare's famous line from *Hamlet* seems to fit as a poke at a sterile absolute naturalism. "There are more things in heaven and earth, Horatio, than are dreamt of in your philosophy." Of course, Hamlet had just been speaking to a ghost in the play. Christians and Israelites have at least occasionally spoken with God, angels or demons. Secular scientists apparently haven't met an angel or demon and probably would not recognize one if it hit them.

The Apostle Paul has a great deal to say about an "outside influencer" toward sin, calling a particular entity "the prince of the power of the air, the spirit that now worketh in the children of disobedience" (Ephesians 2:2). This suggests a kind of "spiritual broadcasting network" that transmits evil attitudes to susceptible people. The "susceptible people" or "children of disobedience" seem to correspond to what Genesis 3:15 calls the "seed" or children of the Serpent (otherwise known as "the Devil" or "Satan" in Revelation 20:2). Now that we know the true identity of the serpent of Eden, we see that the influence to sin and evil even originated in the spirit realm.

So we have evil originating in a sin by our original parents in the Garden of Eden, which seems to somehow have twisted our nature into a kind of distaste for doing God's will at least some of the time. This is apparently reinforced by the outside influence of demonic entities that desire to harm the human race by creating chaos, destruction, war and every other kind of evil that God hates. By influencing us to do evil, demons hope to have us behave in ways that draw God's wrath and punishment upon us.

So what can Jesus do about the problem of evil?

1. Jesus keeps score, and makes things right by punishing evil and rewarding good in the long run.

In Hebrews 4:12-13 we are told something about Jesus, the Word of God. Though not capitalized in the passage, the Word of God is not a passive script that is read, but the Person of Jesus as noted at the beginning of John's Gospel. You can tell this by the context, as the King James Version makes clearer than most other translations.

> *For the word of God is quick [alive], and powerful, and sharper than any two edged sword, piercing even to the dividing asunder of soul and spirit, and of the joints and marrow, and is a discerner of the thoughts and intents of the heart.*
>
> *Neither is there any creature that is not manifest in his sight: but all things are naked and opened unto the eyes of him with whom we have to do.*

Notice how this "word" is able to discern the thoughts and intents of the heart. Jesus is the God to whom we must answer in judgment. The sword of judgment imagery goes back to Joshua 5:12-15. Joshua and Israel have just crossed the Jordan River and are preparing to attack Jericho when a stranger approaches Joshua. This stranger is carrying a sword, and confronts Joshua, who asks if he is for or against Israel. The stranger answers that he is neither for nor against them, but is actually the commander of God's armies. We learn that he is God (the Word, manifested as human) when he tells Joshua to take his shoes off because he is standing on holy ground. (He had done the same thing to Moses.)

God does not let just anyone into His Promised Land, and the sword is symbolic. In other words, to get to Paradise, you have to go through Jesus. If He judges you worthy, you may pass and enter. If not, well, there is a reason Jesus is wielding a sword. You don't want to stick around and watch what He does with it.

Here at the gates of Jericho we can begin to answer some of the charges many have against God: His supposed genocide against the Canaanites. If the Commander of the armies of God is with Joshua and tells him how to attack Jericho, there has already been a judgement on the inhabitants of Jericho. He instructs Joshua to have all of the inhabitants killed.

Where does that come from? How do we know God is punishing them and that the punishment fits the crime? The first clue comes from within a conversation God has with Abraham about Sodom and Gomorrah (Genesis 18:16-33). God tells Abraham that word has reached Him that the cities of the plain, including the two named here, are sinning so egregiously that something has to be done about it. He is sending angels to investigate, and if the reports are true, the cities will be destroyed by divine fire.

Abraham, knowing (as God also knows) that his nephew Lot and Lot's family live there, begins to *negotiate* with God. (Now you know where Jewish people get their *chutzpa* from.) Abraham asks God if He would destroy the cities if 50 "righteous" people were found within the perhaps as many as 2 million residents. God agrees to spare them under those terms. Abraham keeps bringing the number down, *asking if God will judge righteously* by not destroying them if the number is a mere 10.

God agrees not to destroy them if only 10 out of perhaps 2 million are righteous. Unfortunately, the number falls short by 6. Even though the cities are destroyed by fire, the angelic agents of God rescue Lot and his daughters, literally dragging them out by the hands. Only Lot's wife, who had been told not to look back, does not make it to safety. She is turned into a pillar of salt as she turns back in her longing to return to the "civilized" life.

Judge for yourself, but this does not look to me like a God who is randomly genocidal. There must be something so horrible and evil going on, that the only thing left to do is put the population out of its misery, and the only one qualified to do so is the One who created humanity.

A second clue comes from another conversation between God and Abraham, this time about his own descendants. In Genesis 15 God tells Abraham that his descendants will live in a foreign land for 400 years, eventually becoming slaves there and greatly mistreated. God will then judge that nation and release the Abrahamites to bring them to take over the land of Canaan.

So why wait 400 years to bring them to Canaan? God tells Abraham that "the sin of the Amorites has not yet reached its full measure." In other words, God is unwilling to kick out the Canaanites at that time because they are not sinful enough yet, and it will take about 400 years for them to get to the point that they must be removed. God is apparently so *genocidal* that He will have His own people languish in slavery because His enemies are not evil enough yet. Such a hot-tempered God indeed! (Yes, this is what my sarcasm looks like.)

Archaeology has lately discovered what one of those sins seems to have been: child sacrifice. These people would take babies and burn them to death in the red-hot arms of a metal statue of their "god" Molech[xxiv]. They covered the agonized screams of these children with loud drums and trumpets. I doubt that there can be anything so unspeakably evil as *torturing* innocent babies to death in the name of a god. If the entire society condoned that, maybe they did need to be eliminated.

One probably could wonder what God's view on abortion might be, and how that might affect one's nation. Just thinking out loud…

Paul later tells the Athenian Areopagite assembly that the god they had worshiped in ignorance has set a day to judge the world "by the man he has appointed." He continued by saying that the proof of this is that this same man had risen from the dead. In other words, Jesus is the final arbiter and judge of every human being on earth, and will judge the world rightly, in such a way that every human being will understand how correct the judgment is. There is rather chilling imagery of that great last judgment in Revelation 20:11-15.

There is more to say later about that particular judgment and the meaning of being thrown into the lake of fire.

2. Jesus sends representatives to teach people about sin, death and Jesus' mission to redeem humanity from both.

Jesus does not judge without warning people about the result of their sins. For instance, Jesus declares woes on the teachers of the law and Pharisees, warning them of future judgment on them and their nation.

> *Therefore I am sending you prophets and sages and teachers. Some of them you will kill and crucify; others you will flog in your synagogues and pursue from town to town.And so upon you will come all the righteous blood that has been shed on earth, from the blood of righteous Abel to the blood of Zechariah son of Berekiah, whom you murdered between the temple and the altar. - Matthew 23:34-35*

As Jesus is eating his last meal before His death with the disciples, he tells them why He chose them. He says, "When the Advocate comes, whom I will send to you from the Father—the Spirit of truth who goes out from the Father—he will testify about me.

And you also must testify, for you have been with me from the beginning" (John 15:26-27). He later tells them what the Holy Spirit will testify through them.

But very truly I tell you, it is for your good that I am going away. Unless I go away, the Advocate will not come to you; but if I go, I will send him to you. When he comes, he will prove the world to be in the wrong about sin and righteousness and judgment: about sin, because people do not believe in me; about righteousness, because I am going to the Father, where you can see me no longer; and about judgment, because the prince of this world now stands condemned (John 16:5-15).

After His resurrection Jesus tells them once more.

But you will receive power when the Holy Spirit comes on you; and you will be my witnesses in Jerusalem, and in all Judea and Samaria, and to the ends of the earth (Acts 1:8).

That mission continues to this day. All Spirit-led Christians are called to witness to Jesus death, resurrection and continuing Lordship over the world. We also warn people that Jesus is the only One who can offer forgiveness for sin and eternal life. Jesus even made a point of telling the religious authorities in Judea that He has the power to forgive sins, and proved it by healing a paralyzed man by pronouncing forgiveness of his sins (Matthew 9:1-8).

Jesus goes so far as to extend this ability to forgive the sins of others to His disciples (John 20:19-23). In other words, not only are they to proclaim Jesus as the risen Lord and "the Lamb of God who takes away the sin of the world," but they are also in the business of forgiving sin or not forgiving sin on behalf of Jesus. This leads us to the next important way that Jesus deals with the problem of sin.

3. A New Covenant

Back in the section about the book of Jeremiah I discussed an important passage that describes a "new covenant" with Israel and Judah. Jeremiah describes it as follows:

> *The days are coming," declares the LORD, "when I will make a new covenant with the people of Israel and with the people of Judah. It will not be like the covenant I made with their ancestors when I took them by the hand to lead them out of Egypt, because they broke my covenant, though I was a husband to them, " declares the LORD. "This is the covenant I will make with the people of Israel after that time," declares the LORD. "I will put my law in their minds and write it on their hearts. I will be their God, and they will be my people. No longer will they teach their neighbor, or say to one another, 'Know the LORD,' because they will all know me, from the least of them to the greatest," declares the LORD. "For I will forgive their wickedness and will remember their sins no more." (Jeremiah 31:31-34).*

God is predicting a time when His "law" will become integrated into the mind and heart of His people. They will know Him intimately and be obedient to Him. He will forgive them and forget their sins. How can God's law be put into people's hearts?

On the day of Pentecost the disciples receive the Spirit of God (or Holy Spirit) and begin to prophesy (in multiple, known languages). Peter spells out to them what has happened and how they are to respond in Acts 2. They have received the Holy Spirit, which had been promised through the prophet Joel, given by Jesus Christ whom the Jews and Romans had collaborated to crucify.

Peter tells them that they must repent and be baptized in order to receive the Holy Spirit. This process and promise is not only for them, but for all subsequent generations. In Romans 8 Paul gives important information about the Holy Spirit's role and call. The Holy Spirit:

1. Gives life
2. Sets us free from the law of sin and death
3. In you enables you to live according to the desires of the Spirit, not the flesh

4. Living in you means you belong to Christ
5. Is the Spirit of Christ.
6. Raised Christ from the dead will raise anyone in whom He lives
7. Enables those He leads to be children of God
8. Testifies that we are children of God
9. Makes us heirs of Christ, inheriting both His sufferings now and His glory later.

This new covenant is what enables believers to extend forgiveness to people who come to Jesus, repent of their sinful nature and accept Jesus as their Lord and Savior, visibly demonstrating this acceptance of Jesus by water baptism. All of this connects with how Jesus deals with the evil in the world.

To overcome the evil in the world is to root out the evil in the hearts and minds of human beings. The next section will deal with the New Covenant, and how it is different from the Old Covenant. These differences will clarify how the New Covenant deals with the problem of evil.

11

Law and Grace

In the section about origins we discovered that covenant figured very early in the story. We found that the first covenant called that was with Noah and his family and all the animals and their descendants. Since the language was similar to what God had told Adam and Eve, we discerned that God actually had a covenant with them, too.

One of the optional essay topics for a bible college class I attended was to discuss how the Old Testament deals with the concept of "covenant." As I read the scriptures on the subject, I was amazed at how many covenants were actually contained in the Old Testament. Besides Adam and Noah, I identified covenants with Abraham (actually, three of them), Isaac, Jacob, Moses and Israel, the Levitical priesthood, and David. Of course, in the New Testament, Jesus also makes a covenant.

What I have learned since then is that the later covenants overlap with the previous ones, with similarities and differences among them. The defining covenant for Israel was made at Mount Sinai (Exodus 20-23), yet it was based on covenants (yes, plural) with Adam, Noah and Abram/Abraham. Every one of them had a provision that the "covenantees" should be fruitful and multiply, for instance. Each one specified a territory to take care of, such as the Garden of Eden or repopulating the world, or the territory of Canaan.

Even though Gentile Christians were not required to become Jewish in order to become Christians, they still were required to follow the rules of a non-Israelite covenant from God. Acts 15 even reminds Gentile Christians that God had rules for Gentiles from the time of Noah's flood, including a prohibition about eating blood. Jewish and Gentile Christians had to figure out a way to remain in fellowship without harming each others' consciences regarding God's law. It was not easy. And apparently it still isn't.

Here was my own personal dilemma. At the age of 10 I was introduced to the Ten Commandments. This is considered by most Christians to be the basis of Christian morality. Are the Ten Commandments included in the New Covenant? Most Christians believe they are. For those who believe this, the fly in the ointment is the fourth commandment: the Sabbath. Most Christians have been taught that Sunday is now the Sabbath and should be treated as such. I actually once listened to a sermon about sabbath-keeping in a Christian and Missionary Alliance Church in Calgary, using the text from Exodus to announce that we should be keeping Sunday holy!

What a contradiction, since the seventh-day Sabbath of the Bible has no overlap whatsoever with Sunday, the first day of the week! The Roman Catholic Church even claims that God gave them the authority to change the Sabbath to Sunday, according to the Catholic Encyclopedia. They base this claim on Matthew 16:18-19, where Peter appears to be given "the keys to the kingdom," allowing him to bind and loose anything he wants on earth, which will be accepted in heaven. In other words, they changed it according to their own whim - because they could. What is going on here?

These are two attempts to fuse portions of two distinct covenants into a unified whole. I can certainly relate to the desire to do so. Over the years I have even made my own attempts to unify the "old" and "new" covenants, with frustrating results.

Why did I care about a "unified field theory" of God's covenants? This is where my introduction to the work of Herbert W. Armstrong and his Worldwide Church of God comes in. I became a member of that denomination (which many called a cult) for over thirty years. They (and yes, even I) strongly believed that "true" Christians must obey "the Law" in the old Testament. This meant, among other things, that we could not eat pork or certain sea foods. We had to keep the seventh-day Sabbath holy, and this included the spring, summer and autumn festivals of the Old Testament as well. We also believed that Jesus and the Apostles brought new insight into the covenant, such as in Jesus' Sermon on the Mount and Paul and the Jerusalem Council in Acts 15. For instance, I did not rush out to cut off a certain body part because the New Covenant did not require it to be cut off any more.

So, certain parts of the Old Covenant apply in the New Covenant, yet other ones don't? That began to seem strange to the leaders of the denomination after Herbert Armstrong died. They began to send leaders to seminaries to study theology to try to find answers. The answers they found sent shock waves through the denomination and almost completely destroyed it. The answer: the New Covenant completely replaces the Old Covenant. Among other things, there is no longer a Sabbath requirement, and all animal flesh is good for food. Everything that made the organization distinct from other Christian organizations was now *officially wrong*. Imagine the blow to those who believed those things for 40 or more years. We were now "free" to let the "restrictive" old ways die out. We would now meet on Sunday, Easter and Christmas, like all of the other churches.

I did a thought experiment. Assuming that they were correct about the lack of a Sabbath command in the New Covenant, what are we to make of their insistence on gathering on Sunday? The Calgary pastor mentioned above was clearly wrong to insist on keeping Sunday holy. Even the mighty Catholic Church did not have the right to "change" the Sabbath from Saturday to Sunday, since there is no New Covenant Sabbath.

In re-reading the actual Sabbath command I came to realize that it actually said nothing about "gathering" as a community on the Sabbath. All it said is to stop working for that day and simply "rest." Not only that, this command was given to the people of Israel rather than anyone else. My take on that is that Israel was to function as a nation of "priests" to the rest of the world, and therefore had the privilege of being invited to partake of God's Sabbath day of rest. In fact, the "gathering" was *invented* after the exile into Babylon by Jews who wanted to remember God's promises to regather them. They invented the "synagogue," an idea which later was retooled by Christians to become church gathering places. The sabbath gathering and the synagogue were extra-biblical traditions added as a response to Babylonian captivity.

Whether about Saturday or Sunday, the idea of Sabbath rest was already twisted out of its biblical shape by *all churches.* This is not to say that the idea of gathering to worship on an agreed-upon day is inherently wrong. It is just that, even by my denomination's own new logic, requiring a change of gathering day from Saturday to Sunday was not *theologically* necessary. We already had an agreed-upon day to gather - one that had a millennia-long tradition as an appropriate day to worship and take stock of our work.

Since my theological world was now being turned inside out I realized that I needed to study into these matters in greater depth and width for my own sake. I went first to Bible College and later to Seminary to sort out my thinking. It is in this state that I first encountered the depth of Hebrews 8:7-13. The first thing I noticed was that the writer of Hebrews is quoting Jeremiah 31:31-34. Jeremiah 31 is about a restoration of Israel and Judah from exile across many nations. They will not be truly restored until a new covenant is established - one that includes forgiveness of their wickedness and sins. The one quoting notes that *Jeremiah* is speaking about a new covenant, which implies that the old covenant *is already becoming obsolete.* Notice that the writer of Hebrews is saying that *Jeremiah's words* imply that the old covenant is becoming obsolete. So the obvious question that came to me is, *when* was that covenant becoming obsolete?

Was it *becoming* obsolete at the time Hebrews was being written, or *at the time Jeremiah was uttering those words* from the Lord? The fact that God states that a new covenant is both necessary and promised implies that the old covenant is already becoming obsolete. Why? Because God has found fault with the people and is about to kick them out of the Promised Land. He has judged them "guilty" of breach of covenant. The provisions of Deuteronomy 28:58-68 will apply, and they will never be entirely safe in whatever land they find themselves exiled to. That is, until the provisions of Deuteronomy 30:1-8 are met - a "circumcised heart" that causes them to "love him [God] with all your heart and all your soul, and live."

The point that Jeremiah makes in Jeremiah 31:31-34 is that this will be a covenant that is *different from the original covenant with Israel* that was made as they left Egypt. Given that Jeremiah worked until the very destruction of the last Israelite kingdom, this suggests that Jeremiah is saying that the covenant was transitioning to "curses mode." The only way out of the "curse of the law" is to institute a new and radically different covenant.

Through Jesus, God would forgive their *wickedness* and remember their sins no more. Somehow, for many years, I could only process the "sins" part of that statement. Forgiving *wickedness*? How do you *forgive* a deep-rooted, life-long predisposition for evil? How do you forgive *being evil by nature*?

He planned to do so by placing His Spirit in them and thereby "remove" their "heart of stone" and replace it with a "heart of flesh" (Ezekiel 11:19 and 36:26). Once He does this, their nature changes into one of love for and obedience to God. Even though they may have habits that lead to behavior the Bible describes as sin, *sinfulness* (wickedness) is no longer in their nature. Any sinful behavior now becomes contrary to the new nature God has imbued them with, and it now makes the believer miserable.

The new nature, a "circumcised heart," begins to overcome the old inclinations and motivates changes in behavior that would be impossible through simple legalistic observance of the law. This is the essence of the "grace" that was proclaimed by Martin Luther and the other Reformers. Grace is not mere forgiveness. It is also the Spirit-provided ability to reject sinful thoughts and temptations and to overcome learned sinful behavior patterns.

The evil nature has been replaced by a godly nature that now battles the old mental and physical habits as well as the influence of "the spiritual forces of evil in the heavenly realms." (Ephesians 6:12). You are a "new creation" (2 Corinthians 5:17). This means that "the old has gone." The evil part of your nature has been purged and a wholesome new part that loves God has replaced it. *This new nature* is what motivates change of mind and action in accordance with God's will. This is how God "forgives" our "sinfulness." God replaces our sinfulness with His own sinless nature. He describes it as placing His law in our inward parts, as a circumcision of the heart, and as a "heart transplant," - replacing a heart of stone with a heart of flesh, giving us an "undivided heart" and placing a new spirit in us. These are all just poetic ways of describing a spiritual change of heart toward love of, and obedience to, God.

The same theological crisis that started me on this journey of understanding the covenants also had me examine other aspects of biblical teaching. There are other facets that I had to examine about how God deals with the problem of evil. For instance, why do we die? What happens to the dead,? How is unrepentant evil punished and/or destroyed?

Next we will examine death, hell and eternal punishment (the last one is probably not what you think). After that, we will examine eternal life and whether heaven is the reward of the faithful.

12

What are Death and Hell?

This probably seems like a strange question to be asking at this time, but it strikes me as an important one. I could be wrong, but I perceive a great deal of confusion about exactly what death is, as spoken of in the Bible.

Many people seem to have been taught something to the effect that at death they become disembodied spirits who roam around the clouds in heavenly bliss if they are one of the "good" people who don't make God too angry. Of course the "bad" people (almost always someone else) immediately go to a fiery place of endless torment when they die.

Is this what the Bible teaches? Actually, no.

God actually gives a preliminary definition of death early in the Bible. Remember in Genesis 2 that God had told Adam and Eve that if they ate from the tree of the knowledge of good and evil they would surely die. In Genesis 3 the Serpent denies that they would die, but would rather become like God, knowing good and evil.

Once they have taken the fruit God tells Adam, "In the sweat of thy face shalt thou eat bread, till thou return unto the ground; for out of it wast thou taken: for dust thou art, and unto dust shalt thou return."

There you have the definition of death: returning to the ground. God takes soil, shapes it into a human, and breathes life into it. Once he dies, God lets him decompose in the ground and become the soil from which he came. God has de-animated the formerly animated soil. Death is non-life.

As an aside that may become important later, how does God ensure that humans will die? We read that in verses 22-24 of the same chapter. God does not want them to live forever any more, so he banishes them from the garden. Just to make sure they do not try to go back, He sets a guard with a flaming sword to prevent trespassing.

Why eject them from the garden? He banishes them in order to prevent them from eating from the tree of life and live forever. Whatever mysterious life-extending substance or substances the fruit of that tree contains is now lost to humanity, and genetic deterioration begins to set in.

The science geek in me wonders if the fruit from the tree of life contained ingredients that enhance DNA repair and telomere replication. Most of us know what DNA is. If it is not repaired with 100% efficiency defects and eventually even cancers begin to appear in human beings and often in their children. After a number of generations it becomes wise to outlaw marriage by close family members in order to keep the population from multiplying genetic defects by reinforcing damaged genes.

Telomeres are the strands at the end of chromosomes that allow DNA to keep stable while it is opening up to make copies of itself as cells divide. Each split causes the length of the teleomere to shorten. When telomeres become too short, the DNA can no longer make copies of itself. When cells can no longer make copies, cells cannot make new cells to replace dead ones. Tissue repair is prevented and the body ages. This eventually causes death.

So now we are armed with a definition of death and the means by which God enabled it to occur. Have you noticed how physical both the cause and effect are? At this point in the narrative we do not get the sense that anything in a human automatically lives on in another form after death. We are also given a look at the place human beings go when they die: back into the ground.

The Old Testament has a word for that place in its original language: *sheol* (pronounced Shee-ohl). What confuses people is that, like most words in English, it can have literal and metaphorical or poetic non-literal uses.

For instance, you can get descriptions of people being "compassed" (surrounded) by "hell" (*sheol*) as translated by the King James Version in 2 Samuel 22:6. The New International Version translates the same passage as, "the cords of the grave (*sheol*) coiled around me." I have yet to see a grave with tentacles reaching out to catch anyone, so I have to assume that this is a poetic reference to how easy it is to die at the hands of the violent people mentioned in verse 3.

My favorite among the poetic passages is the image in Ezekiel 32:18-28 of the armies ef Elam, Meshech, Tubal and all the others who had dared to fight against God. God is taunting Egypt by telling them to listen to the voices of all of the mighty who tried the same thing. The mighty among the mighty are calling out to them from the grave, preparing a bed in *sheol* for those who are about to die. They are not literally talking from the grave, any more than Abel's blood literally was "crying out from the ground." There is a lot of poetry in the Bible, and you need to understand the kinds of imagery that are being used so masterfully.

Here are some other examples of how *sheol* is used in poetic passages or apocalyptic visions.

Job 17:13 "*the grave is mine house*"

Psalm 30 "*O Lord, thou has brought up my soul from the grave.*" Here David did not actually die. He was prevented from dying, but the emotional response is equivalent to being raised from the dead.

In John's preface to the book of Revelation he states that he was "in the Spirit" on "the Lord's day." This is a flag that what he is experiencing is a series of prophetic visions. The type of visions resemble ones found in the books of Daniel and Ezekiel, which scholars call "apocalyptic." The "day of the Lord" is such a pervasive theme of Old Testament prophetic writings that is surprises me that scholars assume that "the Lord's day" means Sunday, the literal day of the week. To me, that introduction means that John is having visions relating to the Day of the Lord, and that the theme will be the pervasive idea that ties the visions together. But hey, I'm not a scholar, I just have an M. Div. in pastoral ministry. What do I know?

Revelation 6:9-11 describes the faithful dead as souls under the altar. How many souls can fit under an altar? Do they "live" there, or is this a metaphor for their sacrifice on the altar of faith in Jesus Christ? They express a desire for retribution for what has been done to them. After this, they are given robes and told to rest until more are killed. How long do they rest? Apparently until this great tribulation is over and Jesus returns to judge and avenge them all.

Revelation 7:9-17 is vision of people who were killed during "the great tribulation." They are all standing before God and waving palm branches (think Palm Sunday). Clearly this is a vision of the future, since the great tribulation is something that John is to warn Christians about. He wants them to remain faithful no matter what happens to them in the great persecution of Revelation 6:9-11. He is showing the end result of faithfulness to the death.

Here are some passages that describe the "grave condition" of the dead, if you will pardon the pun.

- In Job 7:9 we read, "he that goeth down to the grave shall come up no more."
- Ps. 88:12 describes death as a "the land of oblivion".
- Eccl 9:10 "there is no work, nor device, nor knowledge, nor wisdom, in the grave, whither thou goest."
- Isa. 38:18 "For the grave cannot praise thee, death can not celebrate thee."
- John 11:11-14 Jesus comments that Lazarus is "asleep" and that Jesus plans to "wake" him. When the disciples misunderstand what he means by sleep, Jesus tells them plainly that Lazarus is dead.

From these and many other similar passages one can easily get the impression that death is something like a dreamless sleep. There appears to be no consciousness or activity in the state of being dead.

There are, however, examples of people who seem to have come back in some form from the dead, if only briefly. The first comes from 1 Samuel 28:11-19. King Saul asks a medium to consult with Samuel, who was dead. The medium reports Samuel's words, since only she sees him. Since the story does not challenge the assertion that this is indeed the spirit of Samuel, let us assume that Samuel is the one speaking.

The first thing Samuel says is to ask why Saul has disturbed him by bringing him up. I find this interesting. If he had been conscious and aware, he likely would have known. He seems to have been in some state of unconsciousness until raised to awareness. Once he gives his message that Saul will be joining him soon, we do not hear from Samuel again. God seems to have allowed the medium to speak to Samuel's disembodied "spirit" or "soul" to convey His final message to Saul, at which point Samuel's "soul" goes back to sleep.

However, there may be more to death than a somnolent soul and a decomposing body. We are told in Revelation 20:1-6 and 20:11-15 that there is also a "second death." This death comes after a final judgment that involves punishment. The final punishment, which is called the "second death" is being cast into a lake of fire. "Anyone whose name was not found written in the book of life was thrown into the lake of fire" (vs. 15). The previous verse explains why I call this the "final punishment." I call it that because "death and Hades" are the last to be thrown into the lake of fire. There is no more death or dying after this happens, and therefore no more room for graves or mourning after this judgment and sentence are complete.

Prophets through the ages spoke about God's post-mortem judgment long before Jesus was born. Job asks whether a dead man can live again, and then expresses faith that God will "remember" him and bring him back into His presence (Job 14:14-15). This is what the thief on the cross beside Jesus meant when he asked Jesus to "remember me when you come into your kingdom." (This is such an amazing thing considering that the man he was asking, Jesus, was dying, too.)

David explores the theme of final judgment in Psalm 1:5. "Therefore the wicked will not stand in the judgment, nor sinners in the assembly of the righteous."

In Psalm 73 the prophetic musician, Asaph, notes that the wicked seem to prosper throughout life, while the righteous suffer. He almost loses faith in God until he remembers that there will be a judgment on all human beings. In the end, the wicked will be judged and will perish, but those who fear the Lord will prosper and live.

Later, the writer of Ecclesiastes, whom I have tentatively identified as King Hezekiah of Judah, in 3:17 writes, "I said to myself, 'God will bring into judgment both the righteous and the wicked, for there will be a time for every activity, a time to judge every deed.'"

In Daniel 12:2-3 an angel tells Daniel, "Multitudes who sleep in the dust of the earth will awake: some to everlasting life, others to shame and everlasting contempt. Those who are wise will shine like the brightness of the heavens, and those who lead many to righteousness, like the stars for ever and ever."

So I conclude that when Paul writes, "the wages of sin is death, but the gift of God is eternal life," he is saying that death and life are opposites. The second death is to be avoided because it leads to non-being.

There are only two places in scripture in which *hades* is associated with fire: the parable of Lazarus and the rich man and the time it is cast into the lake of fire in Revelation. We have just discussed the latter as the end of death, so let us examine Lazarus and the rich man.

Because it is not introduced with the word "parable" and one of the individuals involved is given a name, many assume that Jesus is speaking of a real incident rather than employing a parable. Scholars have discovered that similar parables were in circulation around the time of Jesus' ministry. The point that I see most clearly is that it starts with exactly the same words as the previous parable about a rich man's shrewd manager. To me, the words, "There was a rich man…" in both cases suggests a story rather than a real event.

The other thing I notice is that it is in the context of Jesus teaching about the stewardship of money. After Jesus says that you cannot serve both God and money, the Pharisees scoff in derision because they love money. Jesus then launches into a parable about a rich man refusing to share a tiny fraction of his wealth with a poor fellow Jew. God comforts the sufferer and makes the comfortable suffer in some sort of post-mortem judgment.

In case anyone thinks that simply being dead *instead* of being punished forever is not incentive enough to come to Christ, I submit one item of evidence. According to *A World Without Cancer* by Margaret Cuomo, 90 billion dollars have been spent on cancer research and treatment over the past 40 years. Why? People are afraid of dying. Whether Christian or non-Christian, people will spend any amount they can to put death off as long as possible. Even many atheists are afraid to die, even when they do not believe in post-mortem punishment. Non-existence is a frightening prospect, even by itself.

Jesus says that eternal life is His to grant. Do not be fooled by the idea that your soul will automatically live on forever. That was Satan's lie. In Matthew 10:28 Jesus says that you should "fear the one who can destroy both body and soul in hell (*gehenna,* the lake of fire)." Do not be fooled by the scientists and even theologians who believe Jesus either did not exist or was not accurately described by the disciples and their followers.

Jesus is real. He rules the universe. He will judge every human being who ever has and will live. Remember that "The fear of the LORD is the beginning of knowledge, but fools despise wisdom and instruction." (Proverbs 1:7). Proverbs 9:10 also notes that the fear of the LORD is the beginning of wisdom, too. Be wise.

Now we see that "hell" can describe the grave with the Hebrew word *sheol* and the Greek word *hades*. The other Greek word, *gehenna,* refers to a future judgment culminating in being destroyed in a "lake of fire." There is a further Greek word, *tartaros*, which refers to a kind of "holding cell" for corrupted angelic beings or demons until their time of judgment. We have also learned that death is primarily a state of non-consciousness in the grave, that is followed by a final judgment that may lead to a final erasure of conscious existence if warranted.

On the other hand, those found in the "book of life" have a different fate. Now that we have a better idea of what death and hell are, let us discuss "heaven."

13

Heaven and Salvation

The word "gospel" is a contraction of the older English expression god spell, which meant "good news." The previous section primarily was about the "bad news" about what happens to unrepentant sinners who fail God's judgment. The "good news" is about the way to not only avoid the ultimate destruction of your being in the "lake of fire," but about its wonderful alternative: eternal life.

Like our English word "hell," the Greek and Hebrew words representing the concept of "heaven" carry a range of possible meanings. In Genesis 1 it refers broadly to the cosmos or observable universe. Any time you see the word pluralized you can assume that is what is being referred to. "Heaven," singular, can refer either to what we call the portion of the sky containing our atmosphere (where birds fly, for instance) or the other-worldly realm that contains God's temple, throne room and court. God's heaven seems not to be observable from earth, and may exist invisibly alongside it in the sky or simply outside of the universe as we know it.

Throughout a lot of the history of the church, many Christians have held some version of the idea that the "soul" or "spirit" of human beings who have found favor with God go up to heaven when the body dies. This concept seems to be tied tightly to the idea that human beings have immortal souls. Whether or not we have immortal souls, Jesus Himself does not seem to agree that the good ones automatically go to heaven.

Before Jesus came to earth nobody went to God's heaven. He says so in John 3:13, "No one has gone to heaven except the one who came from heaven -

the Son of Man." Of course, some may argue that nobody could go to heaven until Jesus completed His mission and salvation was available to all. That is an interesting theory that may have evidence in the vision of the fifth seal of Revelation 6:9-11. Souls of those beheaded for Christ are seen under the altar before God's throne room. Remember that John is experiencing a series of visions, and that they may be grounded in a truth that is not necessarily literal, but rather symbolic.

What about those who died of natural causes? We have no information about them going to heaven as soon as they die. On the other hand, on the 50th day after Jesus' resurrection Peter notes that not even King David has gone to heaven (Acts 2:34). Was David's paperwork not up to date? And where is the "bosom of Abraham" that Lazarus was supposed to go to when he and the rich man died? Many questions about this do not have the definitive answers we want from the Bible.

Here is the most open secret you learn when going to seminary. *No seminary professor who is a true Christian believes that the Bible teaches that being a disembodied soul in heaven is the reward of the saved.* Every one that I have met understands that Jesus teaches the *bodily resurrection* of the faithful to eternal life (1 Corinthians 15:20-23).

When Jesus returns to earth, He calls His people to meet Him in the air (1 Thessalonians 4:16-18) and they will be with Him forever. Those who died for Jesus' name will rule with Jesus for 1000 years on earth (Revelation 20:4-6) while Satan is bound in a bottomless pit (20:1-3). So at this point we see the faithful resurrected and residing on earth for at least 1000 years. These people are already given eternal life and therefore will never suffer the "second death" that some others may suffer in the final judgment. More on that second death later.

After Satan is released for a brief time and causes a massive rebellion, he will be cast into the same lake of fire the Beast and False Prophet had been cast into a millennium before (verses 7-10). This is followed by a Great Judgment before a White Throne. Note that, until that point, only three entities have been cast into that lake. The rest of the armies have been destroyed in both cases either by plague (pre-millennial) or by fire (post-millennial).

There is a Great White Throne Judgment. The ones not found in the Book of Life are judged and found guilty. They are *then* cast into the Lake of Fire, followed by death and *hades*. Following this, God creates a *new heavens and a new earth.* We are told that there is then no more death or mourning. This means that the fire even *destroyed* ***death***.

A new heavens and new earth means that there is no more "place" for death or "hell," whether the grave or the fiery *gehenna.* "The old order of things has passed away." Says Jesus, "I am making all things new."

It is on this new earth that the survivors of God's judgment live forever, with a New Jerusalem as its earthly capitol (Revelation 21 and 22). The tree of life has multiplied along the river of water of life within the New Jerusalem, making it look a lot like an urbanized version of the Garden of Eden. This suggests that the human race has been given a re-boot with all of the "bugs" finally fixed. Humanity can now truly fulfill God's will of taking care of His creation. People of all the "nations" frequently come to Jerusalem to worship the Lamb and the Father. All people are holy and obedient to God, while happily engaged in managing the welfare of all the creatures on the earth.

So, is heaven the reward of the saved? Certainly not as disembodied souls. The reward of the saved is resurrection to eternal life, ultimately in a very earthly paradise. The presence of God's throne in Jerusalem, with God (the Father) and the Lamb seated on it suggest, if anything, that heaven has come to earth.

Conclusion

As a Christian, I am convinced that the Bible has very important things to tell us about the reality we live in. We live in a world with both physical and spiritual elements. Spiritual elements can only be discerned by spiritual means, which means that science, as modern people have defined it, cannot draw conclusions about it. Definitions, by nature, are limiting.

Ancient peoples had a different view of science. "Science" meant knowledge and included *any* accumulated knowledge of the world around them, including the spiritual. Morality and ethics are not physical properties, for instance, and cannot rationally be "discovered" by science. They can and have been, however, *revealed* by spiritual insight from spiritual sources. For both Jews and Christians, the great giver of moral law is the One God who interacted with Moses and the people of Israel.

That same God also created and maintains the physical universe, including the earth we live on. How do we know? ***God told us!***

God told the whole congregation of Israel at Mount Sinai about the six days of creation as part of the Sabbath Commandment in Exodus 20. This was a condensed form of Genesis 1, involving the very number of days that it took for God to create all that we can see today. We are blessed that Moses had the presence of mind to copy what God had written on the stone tablets of the Law before it was seemingly irretrievably lost in the Babylonian invasion.

We are also blessed that so many people, spanning most of early human history, have recorded their observations of events around them and their interactions with the God of Abraham, Isaac and Israel. This includes those who interacted with Jesus of Nazareth, the Anointed One (the meaning of "Christ"), the Son of God. These were honest writers who were not afraid to let everyone know their bias in favor of God and Jesus, unlike many "unbiased" scholars and scientists today.

There is a bias against the God of the Bible and against Christians in our modern scientific and political realms in the Western world today. Evolution sounds scientific but denies a great deal of evidence in favor of creation by divine fiat. Politicians cite "tolerance" to deny tolerance to Christian values. The former is a definite bias, and the latter is outright hypocrisy.

I have pointed out some of the evidence that evolutionary theory is based more on anti-God conjecture than on real evidence. There is evidence that earth has existed for a far shorter time than the billions of years that is ignored or rationalized away by those who do not want a Creator. Carbon 14 in dinosaur bones and coal deposits is certainly not evidence of millions of years, for instance. Truth can be found anywhere you look, if you have the eyes to see.

The Bible is not anti-scientific but can rather inform scientists with ways of testing its veracity. Learning that the "waters below" were" gathered in one place" helps us see that there originally was only one (super)continent. Understanding the breaking open of the "fountains of the deep" has led to the theory of "catastrophic plate tectonics," which helps us understand such things as the score marks on the ocean bottoms and the relatively cool temperature of rock that slipped under the continental plates.

The "fountains of the deep" can also represent the lava flows on land and under the ocean that created the conditions necessary for a global ice age after the biblical flood. The water had to be warm for high evaporation, with "nuclear winter" sized cloud-cover, making the land relatively cool for maximum precipitation of snow.

The notion that God created earth and the planetary bodies out of water led to a testable theory about collapsing planetary magnetic fields. This led to a prediction by Dr. Humphries about the strength of magnetic fields of planets with liquid cores. The accuracy of his field strength calculations was later confirmed by the Voyager 1 and 2 space probes.

All of these are instances of God giving enough information to show His work as Creator. These are only a few of the remarkable observations that have been made by believing scientists and observers over the last few years. The information is out there, all over the internet for those with eyes to see. The Apostle Paul writes,

> *For since the creation of the world God's invisible qualities—his eternal power and divine nature—have been clearly seen, being understood from what has been made, so that people are without excuse. For although they knew God, they neither glorified him as God nor gave thanks to him, but their thinking became futile and their foolish hearts were darkened. Although they claimed to be wise, they became fools and exchanged the glory of the immortal God for images made to look like a mortal human being and birds and animals and reptiles. (Romans 1:20-23 NIV)*

For those unfamiliar with the Bible, I also tried to provide an overview of how the Bible is organized. I outlined different types of writing or "genres" in the Bible. This was to help you understand *how to read* the different styles. I also gave a brief summary of the contents of different books of the Bible.

The next several sections covered what amounts to the overall history recorded in the Bible, with my own commentary about the intersection of scripture, history and science. I went through the creation, The (one and only) human race and our common beginning as the family of Adam. We covered the spiritual wickedness that began with disobedience by Adam and Eve and culminated in the worldwide flood at the time of Noah.

This was followed by the consequences of the rescue of Noah and his family on post-flood humanity, leading to a genetic bottleneck and an overall shortened human lifespan. We covered the division of the world into distinct languages and cultures at the Tower of Babel. These cultures were scattered around the world and left under the auspices of angelic beings, since they had rejected God to build their own civilization.

God then begins the process of calling people back to Him through choosing Abram and promising him a nation and blessings. This includes supernaturally creating a nation through a couple that could not bear children. From Abraham we moved into the history of his family. God promises that the tribe of Judah would eventually produce a great king who would rule a peaceful nation in perpetuity.

In the meantime, they reside in Egypt, eventually becoming oppressed slaves. God frees them with mighty miracles and became a nation in the wilderness under the leadership of God through the great prophet Moses. God makes a covenant with the nation at Mount Sinai and they eventually enter the Promised Land.

From there we covered Israel's rise and fall through the Judges and the later Kings. King David becomes the prototype of the Priest/King that was predicted to come from Judah, but he and his descendants each have fatal flaws that prevent the full establishment of the perpetual kingdom. Israel splits in two, and both parts eventually fall to foreign invaders who carry them away into captivity.

God's covenant, however, promises that there will always be a remnant scattered among the nations who remember their origin and restoration under certain conditions. From these scattered people God would still produce the promised King. Centuries pass, and this promise is fulfilled by God in human form: Jesus Christ, the Son of God.

Jesus solves the problem of death by dying for our sins and living again to be our great High Priest. Through the payment for our sins, He can offer forgiveness and follow that up with eternal life through the promise of resurrection from the dead. We can have confidence in the promise because Jesus was dead, and is now alive forever. We have been given reliable eyewitness accounts and a compiled biography.

Jesus continues His ministry even after his rising up to heaven. He becomes King of Kings, ruling over those who believe in Him. He provides the Holy Spirit to His disciples on the day of Pentecost. Later, He literally recruits Saul to evangelize the Roman world. How else was it possible for Christianity to become the largest religion in the world?

Jesus solves the problem of evil. First, He is Judge of the living and the dead. He rewards and punishes with perfect justice those who commit themselves to evil acts. He also forgives those who repent and come to Him for forgiveness, giving them a new heart and turning them away from the desire to do evil. You can do away with evil by doing away with the evil-doers or changing the evil-doers into doers of good. Jesus does both as needed.

Finally, I went over different erroneous or unproven ideas that have been promoted, usually by well-meaning Christian writers. These topics included death, hell and heaven.

Death is like a holding cell, a place for dead bodies and souls that are basically unconscious until it is time for God to either reward or judge. There have been instances in which dead people appear in either non-physical form or visions, but these are rare and only seem to occur when God has a specific purpose, such as showing Jesus' glory to the disciples or predicting King Saul's demise.

The term "hell" is an English word that covers three meanings. The first is what we can refer to as "the grave" or the resting place of the dead. Hell also refers to a holding place for rebellious angelic or demonic beings where they are "reserved in chains" while awaiting judgment. Finally, hell also can refer to the "lake of fire and brimstone" described in Revelation, which is the final fate of those who refuse to accept Jesus as Lord and savior. This last "hell" seems to extinguish the existence of "both body and soul" as Jesus warns.

In other words, the idea of an eternal burning torment for rebellious humans seems to have been perversely read into the Bible rather than taken from the Bible. So far as we can read, the eternal torment seems to be restricted to supernatural entities such as those called the Beast, the False Prophet and the Devil.

Finally, the idea of going to heaven as disembodied "immortal souls" misrepresents the seriousness of death as our enemy. We do not automatically get to heaven, even if we are martyrs. For one thing, the saints are resurrected bodily when Jesus returns, not before. Even if there are martyred "souls" in heaven, they return to new bodies when Jesus comes to earth, and even rule with Him for one thousand years on earth.

After the Great White Throne Judgment, with Jesus as Judge, a new earth is created, and all remaining humanity dwells there, with Jerusalem the world capital city. Humanity does not go to heaven so much as heaven comes to earth. Jesus will dwell on earth with humanity forever!

It is my prayer and hope that this book has given you a greater appreciation and perspective about the reliability of the Bible and the truly good news about Jesus the Creator, Redeemer and King of Kings as presented within it.

Resources

The following are books that I found helpful in gaining perspective on the soundness of the Bible's information regarding science and the creation.

1) *Darwin's Black Box: The Biochemical Challenge to Evolution* by Michael J. Behe. Touchstone Books, New York, 1998.

> *Behe digs down into biochemistry to show how some biochemical functions have an "irreducible complexity" that make it impossible for them to have functioned without all of the parts already intact. In other words, there is no way to go from a simpler version with only some of the parts to one that functions at all, let alone efficiently.*

2) *Evolution's Achilles' Heels*, Edited by Robert Carter, Ph D. Creation Book Publishers, Powder Springs, 2005.

> *Nine Ph D scientists and philosophers take on all of the supposedly strongest arguments for the theory of evolution and point out the fatal flaws of each one. Subjects covered are 1) Natural Selection, 2) Genetics and DNA, 3) the Origin of Life, 4) the Fossil Record, 5) the Geologic Record, 6) Radiometric Dating, 7) Cosmology, and 8) Ethics and Morality.*

3) *The Fire That Consumes: A Biblical and Historical Study of the Doctrine of Final Punishment*, by Edward William Fudge. Cascade Books, Eugene, 2011.

> *A monumental and truly biblical look at what the scriptures actually teach about the final end of the wicked, and the language of destruction used throughout. This is the most thoroughly researched book about the subject available.*

4) *The Challenge of Jesus: Rediscovering Who Jesus Was and Is*, by N.T. Wright. Intervarsity Press, Downer's Grove, 1999.

Unlike many scholars who want to debunk Jesus Christ as the true Son of God, Anglican bishop and New Testament scholar N.T. Wright brings us back to solid ground with many excellent reasons to believe that Jesus is exactly who His disciples believed He was and is.

5) wascanafellowship.wordpress.com

This one is my blog, in which I bring together other information about the Bible, including a paper I wrote about hell, God's covenants, the book of Revelation and other musings about Jesus, Christianity and the Bible. You are welcome to leave any feedback, comment or critique. I may, of course, edit or delete any outrageously crude or profane language or spam content.

I do not pretend to be infallible or all-knowing about these subjects. If you have any questions, comments or criticisms about this book or any other related subject I can be reached by email at wjvalade@sasktel.net.

Notes

[i] Mark 6:3 '"Isn't this the carpenter? Isn't this Mary's son and the brother of James, Joseph, Judas and Simon? Aren't his sisters here with us?" And they took offense at him.'

[ii] Matthew 8:14 'When Jesus came into Peter's house, he saw Peter's mother-in-law lying in bed with a fever.' Peter's mother-in-law mentioned in Mark 1:30 and Luke 4:38.

[iii] 1 Corinthians 9:5 'Don't we have the right to take a believing wife along with us, as do the other apostles and the Lord's brothers and Cephas ?' Cephas is another name for Peter. The point is that some apostles brought their wives with them on their missionary journeys. This suggests that a celibate priesthood is not what God had in mind for His church.

[iv] https://en.wikipedia.org/wiki/Gregor_Mendel

[v] https://en.wikipedia.org/wiki/Reading_frame 'DNA encodes protein sequence by a series of three-nucleotide codons. Any given sequence of DNA can therefore be read in six different ways: Three reading frames in one direction (starting at different nucleotides) and three in the opposite direction.'

[vi] https://pandemictimeline.com/wp-content/uploads/2021/08/Pfizer-bio-distribution-confidential-document-translated-to-english.pdf This document was controversial because it was not released to the general public by Phizer, but rather informally to researchers who requested it. The percentages of actual mRNA distributed widely are small, but this was not expected to happen at all.

[vii] https://www.cdc.gov/coronavirus/2019-ncov/vaccines/different-vaccines/mrna.html Note that they expected the spike protein to stick to the cell wall.

[viii] https://newsrescue.com/stanford-study-finds-cytotoxic-spike-protein-level-in-vaccinees-overlaps-with-the-range-of-spike-antigen-in-acute-infection/ This study contradicts the expectation that spike protein exclusively sticks to the cell wall. It finds its way into the bloodstream in quantities comparable to Covid spike proteins in sick patients.

[ix] Evolution's Achilles' Heels, pp. 196-198

[x] https://wascanafellowship.wordpress.com/2016/07/26/for-in-six-days-the-lord-made-the-heavens-and-the-earth/

[xi] Evolution's Achilles' Heels, pp. 206-209

[xii] Evolution's Achilles' Heels, p. 209.

[xiii] https://coldcasechristianity.com/writings/is-there-any-evidence-for-jesus-outside-the-bible/

[xiv] The essay, New Testament Use of the Old Testament by Roger Nicole is reproduced from *Revelation and the Bible*, ed. Carl. F.H. Henry (Grand Rapids: Baker, 1958), pp. 137-151. Roger Nicole notes that he has counted 224 direct quotes from the Old Testament in the New Testament. According to him, others have counted from 613 to as many as 4105 allusions to Old Testament passages in the New Testament alone. [This does not include the number of times Old Testament writers quote or allude to other Old Testament writings.]

[xv] https://en.wikipedia.org/wiki/Miller%E2%80%93Urey_experiment

[xvi] Problems with the experimental design of Miller-Urey. https://bigthink.com/hard-science/miller-urey/

[xvii] The first three chapters explain the problems not addressed by milller-ursey and others since: www.discovery.org/a/24041/

[xviii] Spike Psarris, What You Aren't Being Told About Astronomy, Volume II: Our Created Stars and Galaxies. Video presentation that provides the information found in the this and the following nine paragraphs.

[xix] Evolution's Achilles' Heels, p. 230..

[xx] *Evolution's Achilles' Heels*, Ed. Robert Carter. Powder Springs: Creation Book Publishers, 2015.

[xxi] "Spirit Lake and the Floating Log Mat." From the YouTube site Is Genesis History? Watch it at https://www.youtube.com/watch?v=LjA-jYEWlwU

[xxii] "Spirit Lake and the Floating Log Mat." From the YouTube site Is Genesis History? Watch it at https://www.youtube.com/watch?v=LjA-jYEWlwU

[xxiii] Wikipedia has a page about Utnapishtim and his boxy "ark":https://en.wikipedia.org/wiki/Utnaposhtim

[xxiv] 2 Kings 23:10 compare with Jeremiah 7:31. More information at: https://allthatsinteresting.com/moloch

For author interviews or more information contact:

John Valade
C/O Advantage Books
info@advbooks.com

To purchase additional copies of these books, visit our bookstore at
www.advbookstore.com

Orlando, Florida, USA
"we bring dreams to life"™
www.advbookstore.com

www.ingramcontent.com/pod-product-compliance
Lightning Source LLC
LaVergne TN
LVHW050638100826
845148LV00011B/1895

9781597557245